Liquidity & Runway

How to Build Financial Time, Extend Your Runway, and Stay Stable in an Unstable Economy

MARK ELLISON

PERENNIAL PUBLISHING

Published by Perennial Publishing

First Edition

Paperback ISBN: 978-971996-12-7
Hardcover ISBN: 978-971996-13-4
EBook ISBN: 978-971996-14-1

For bulk or institutional orders, contact Perennial Publishing.

Contents

Introduction

Financial stability is often interpreted through visible financial metrics. Income, in particular, is treated as the primary measure of financial strength. Higher income is widely assumed to produce greater stability, while lower income is assumed to produce vulnerability. Budgets, financial advice, and public discussions of personal finance frequently revolve around the idea that increasing income is the central path toward financial security.

This assumption appears reasonable because income represents the flow of resources entering a household's financial system. Income pays for housing, food, transportation, and every other recurring obligation that structures daily life. When income rises, households appear to gain capacity. When income falls, pressure immediately becomes visible.

Yet income alone does not fully explain why some households remain stable through disruption while others experience rapid financial stress.

Two households with similar income levels can experience very different financial outcomes when conditions change. One household absorbs disturbances gradually while maintaining operational stability. Another encounters immediate pressure when income is interrupted or when expenses unexpectedly increase. In these moments, the difference between stability and instability is rarely explained by income alone.

The missing variable is financial time.

Financial systems behave differently depending on how much financial time exists between the appearance of a disturbance and the moment when a response becomes unavoidable. This time determines whether decisions are made carefully or under pressure. It determines whether financial adjustments occur gradually or must be implemented immediately.

Liquidity is the mechanism that creates this time.

Understanding how liquidity converts money into time, and how that time governs financial stability, is the central focus of this book.

Income occupies a central position in most discussions of household finance. It is measurable, visible, and easy to compare. Paychecks arrive at regular intervals, annual salaries can be calculated precisely, and increases in income are widely understood as improvements in financial strength.

Because of this clarity, income is often treated as the primary determinant of financial stability.

When financial stress appears, the explanation frequently returns to income levels. A household may be described as struggling because income is too low relative to expenses. Conversely, households with higher earnings are commonly assumed to possess greater resilience simply because their inflows of money are larger.

This framework captures an important part of the financial system, but it remains incomplete.

Income represents a flow of resources entering the household. It determines the scale at which the financial system operates. However, it does not fully determine how the system behaves when conditions change.

Financial disturbances occur regularly in household life. Employment transitions, reductions in working hours, unexpected expenses, and health events interrupt normal financial patterns. These disturbances may be temporary, but their effects depend on how the household financial structure absorbs them.

Income alone does not determine this response.

Two households earning similar incomes may experience the same disturbance — a temporary interruption in income, for example. One household reorganizes its financial structure and continues operating with minimal disruption. The other experiences immediate financial pressure that spreads rapidly across obligations.

From the perspective of income, the two systems appear similar. From the perspective of stability, they behave very differently.

The reason lies in how the financial structure is configured around the flow of income.

Income typically arrives on a predictable schedule, while expenses must be paid on specific dates. Housing payments, utilities, insurance, and other obligations occur according to fixed timelines. These timelines continue regardless of whether income flows smoothly or temporarily stops.

When income flows uninterrupted, this structure functions normally. When income becomes uncertain, however, the timing of obligations becomes critical.

If a household lacks the ability to continue meeting obligations during an interruption, even a brief disruption can produce immediate stress. Bills arrive before solutions can be implemented. Obligations accumulate faster than the household can adjust.

In these circumstances, the financial system does not fail because income is insufficient in the long term. It fails because the system lacks the ability to operate long enough for adjustments to occur.

Income therefore determines the scale of the financial system, but it does not determine how much time the system has to respond when disturbances appear.

Without time, even small disruptions can destabilize the structure.

With time, larger disruptions can often be absorbed without permanent damage.

Understanding household financial stability therefore requires moving beyond income as the sole indicator of strength and examining the temporal structure that surrounds it.

That temporal structure is where liquidity becomes central.

In most financial discussions, time appears indirectly. Loan terms are measured in years, investments are evaluated over long horizons, and budgets are often described monthly. Yet these references to time do not capture the role that time plays during financial disruption.

The critical function of time emerges when disturbance interrupts the normal flow of income.

When income changes suddenly — whether through employment transitions, reduced hours, or unexpected expenses — the household must respond. Expenses may need to be adjusted, obligations reorganized, or new income sources established.

All of these adjustments require time.

The stability of the financial system therefore depends not only on the resources available but also on the amount of time the household possesses to implement these adjustments.

This time determines how disturbances are experienced.

When reaction time is sufficient, financial disturbances unfold gradually. Households can observe conditions, evaluate alternatives, and implement changes deliberately. Obligations continue to be met while the adjustment process occurs.

When reaction time is limited, disturbances accelerate. Bills continue to arrive on schedule while solutions remain uncertain. The household must make decisions immediately in order to maintain operational continuity.

The difference between these two situations is not necessarily the size of the disturbance itself. Instead, it is the amount of time available to respond.

Consider two households experiencing the same temporary income interruption. If one household has several months of operational flexibility, it can search for new income, reorganize expenses, and respond deliberately. The disturbance remains contained within the system.

If the other household can operate only for a few weeks without income, the same interruption becomes urgent. Obligations approach quickly, and decisions must be made before full information is available.

In this environment, the financial system begins to operate under pressure rather than analysis.

Financial time therefore acts as a stabilizing variable within household finance.

When time is abundant, disturbances are distributed across a longer adjustment period. When time is scarce, disturbances concentrate rapidly and produce cascading pressure across the financial structure.

This role of time is rarely emphasized because it is less visible than income or expenses. Reaction time cannot be observed directly in a bank statement. It becomes visible only when disruption occurs.

Yet when disruption does occur, time becomes the governing variable that determines how the financial system behaves.

Households with sufficient reaction time retain control over the sequence and quality of financial decisions. Households without reaction time must respond immediately to external pressure.

The question then becomes how households create this reaction time within their financial structures.

The answer lies in liquidity.

Liquidity is commonly defined as money that can be accessed quickly. Cash, bank balances, and other immediately available funds fall into this category because they are usable without delay.

This definition identifies the form of liquidity but not its functional role within a household financial system.

Liquidity performs a structural function: it converts money into time.

When income flows normally, liquidity often appears passive. Funds remain unused while obligations are paid through regular income. Because liquidity is rarely needed during stable periods, it can appear secondary to income itself.

However, the importance of liquidity becomes clear when financial disturbances occur.

When income is interrupted or expenses increase unexpectedly, households must continue meeting obligations while they reorganize their financial structure. Housing payments, utilities, and essential expenses continue regardless of the disturbance.

Liquidity allows these obligations to be met while adjustments are underway.

In effect, liquidity extends the operating time of the financial system.

Rather than requiring immediate solutions, the household gains the ability to continue functioning while evaluating options. Expenses can still be paid while new income is located or obligations are renegotiated. The system remains operational during the adjustment process.

This extension of time is what converts liquidity into financial time.

Without liquidity, the household must respond immediately to disturbances because obligations cannot be postponed. Bills must be paid as they arrive, and the absence of available funds compresses the time available for decision-making.

With liquidity, the household gains a buffer between disturbance and response. Financial pressure is absorbed temporarily while adjustments are considered.

This buffering process slows the propagation of shocks.

Instead of spreading immediately across the financial structure, disturbances are absorbed and distributed across time. The household gains the ability to evaluate options carefully and implement responses sequentially rather than simultaneously.

Liquidity therefore performs the role of a shock absorber within household finance.

It does not prevent disturbances from occurring. Income interruptions and unexpected expenses remain unavoidable features of financial life. Instead, liquidity determines how quickly those disturbances propagate through the financial structure.

When liquidity is present, disturbances move slowly and remain manageable. When liquidity is absent, disturbances move rapidly and produce immediate pressure.

This difference in propagation speed determines whether financial systems remain stable during disruption.

Liquidity does not simply represent available money. It represents the amount of time the financial system can continue operating while problems are solved.

Understanding liquidity as financial time therefore reveals why it plays such a central role in household financial stability.

If financial stability depends on time, then the structure of that time becomes the central question for household finance.

Time determines whether disturbances remain manageable or escalate into crisis. It determines whether decisions can be evaluated carefully or must be made under immediate pressure. Ultimately, it determines whether the financial system retains stability when conditions change.

Liquidity is the mechanism that creates this time.

However, liquidity itself must be understood within a broader structural concept: financial runway.

Financial runway refers to the length of time a household can continue meeting essential obligations if income becomes uncertain or temporarily interrupted. It measures how long the financial system can operate before structural adjustments become unavoidable.

In practical terms, financial runway represents the duration between the moment income is disrupted and the moment when obligations can no longer be met without structural change.

This duration governs the household's decision environment.

When financial runway is long, households possess substantial financial time. They can observe economic conditions, search for new income sources, renegotiate obligations, or reorganize expenses gradually. The system retains stability during the adjustment process.

When financial runway is short, reaction time disappears. Obligations approach quickly, and decisions must be made immediately. The financial system enters a compressed decision environment where urgency dominates evaluation.

The consequences of this compression extend beyond the initial disturbance. Decisions made under pressure often introduce new structural obligations that persist long after the original problem has been resolved.

For this reason, financial runway functions as a governing variable in household finance.

It connects liquidity to decision quality and decision quality to long-term stability. The longer the runway, the more time households possess to respond deliberately to uncertainty. The shorter the runway, the more rapidly financial pressure accumulates.

The central purpose of this book is to examine how financial runway is constructed within household financial systems.

The chapters that follow explore how households build liquidity, how financial runway can be measured, how it changes over time, and how different financial structures influence the length of available reaction time.

By examining liquidity through the lens of time, a clearer understanding of financial stability begins to emerge.

Households do not maintain stability simply because income is high or expenses are controlled. They maintain stability because their financial structures produce sufficient financial time to manage uncertainty.

This leads to the central question that guides the book:

If financial stability depends on time, how do households build, measure, and protect financial runway?

The Hidden Variable Behind Financial Stability

Household finance is commonly evaluated through a small set of visible indicators. Income is the most prominent. Salary levels, hourly wages, and annual earnings are treated as primary markers of financial strength. When income rises, stability is assumed to follow. When income falls, instability is expected to emerge.

This framework appears intuitive, but it overlooks a variable that is rarely measured directly: financial time.

Financial time determines how households experience financial pressure. It determines whether problems can be managed gradually or must be resolved immediately. It determines whether households operate from stability or from urgency.

Income alone does not determine these conditions.

Two households can earn identical incomes and yet experience completely different levels of financial stability. Both may receive the same paycheck, pay similar housing costs, and maintain comparable monthly expenses. From the outside, their financial structures appear nearly identical.

Yet when disruption occurs — a delayed paycheck, a job transition, a medical bill, a temporary reduction in hours — their outcomes diverge.

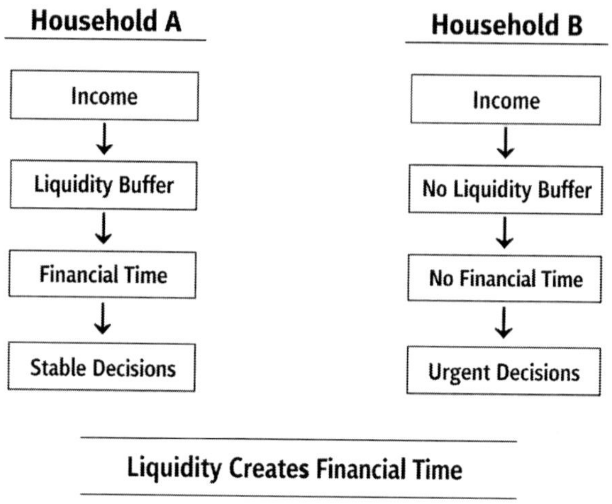

[Diagram 1 - Income vs Financial Time]

One household adjusts. Payments are reorganized, expenses are delayed, and the disturbance is absorbed without structural damage.

The other household enters immediate stress. Bills must be paid within days. Choices must be made quickly. Borrowing becomes necessary. The disturbance spreads across the entire financial structure.

The difference between these households is not income.

The difference is time.

It determines how long a household can continue operating while a problem is being addressed. It determines whether decisions are made deliberately or under pressure.

In financial systems, time is created through liquidity.

Liquidity refers to resources that can be used immediately without restructuring assets or taking on additional obligations. It represents the portion of a household's financial structure that is available to absorb shocks.

When liquidity is present, financial time expands. Households can wait, evaluate, and adjust.

When liquidity is absent, financial time collapses. Decisions must occur quickly because obligations cannot be postponed.

This difference in available time fundamentally alters the stability of a household's financial system.

Without liquidity, every disruption becomes urgent. Income interruptions immediately threaten bill payments. Unexpected expenses cannot be absorbed.

With liquidity, disruptions slow down. Obligations can still be met while households evaluate alternatives.

In this way, liquidity acts as the hidden variable of household finance.

Income determines the scale of resources entering the system. Expenses determine the rate at which those resources leave. But liquidity determines how much time the system has to respond when conditions change.

This distinction is often overlooked because income is visible while time is not. Paychecks can be measured. Budgets can be calculated. But reaction time — the ability to continue operating when income becomes uncertain — is rarely considered directly.

Yet reaction time is what determines whether a financial disturbance becomes a temporary inconvenience or a destabilizing event.

Understanding household finance therefore requires shifting focus from income alone to the time structure that income supports.

Liquidity creates that structure.

It transforms money from a static quantity into operational time.

And that time determines whether financial systems remain stable when uncertainty inevitably arrives.

Liquidity is often described as cash or easily accessible funds. While this definition is technically correct, it does not fully explain the role liquidity plays inside a household financial system.

Liquidity performs a more important function: it converts money into time.

Money by itself is a quantity. It represents accumulated resources. Liquidity determines how those resources interact with time when income becomes uncertain or interrupted.

To understand this mechanism, it is useful to introduce the concept of financial runway.

Financial runway refers to the amount of time a household can continue operating if income is reduced or temporarily lost. It measures how long essential expenses can be covered before the financial system begins to fail.

Runway is therefore a time metric, not a dollar metric.

Two households may each hold $15,000 in liquid savings. If one household's monthly expenses are $3,000 and the other's are $7,500, their financial runway differs substantially. The first household has roughly five months of operational time. The second has only two.

The same amount of money produces different amounts of time depending on the structure of the financial system.

This relationship highlights the true role liquidity plays. Liquidity does not merely represent available funds; it represents the time a household can operate while uncertainty is resolved.

In stable periods, this time may appear unnecessary. Income flows regularly, bills are paid on schedule, and liquidity remains unused. Because the liquidity is rarely touched, it may seem passive or redundant.

However, its function becomes clear when disruption occurs.

Income interruptions are a normal feature of financial life. Job transitions occur. Hours fluctuate. Businesses experience slow periods. Health events interrupt work. Economic conditions change.

When these disturbances appear, households must adjust their financial structure. They may search for new employment, renegotiate obligations, reduce discretionary spending, or temporarily reorganize priorities.

All of these adjustments require time.

Liquidity provides the financial time necessary for those adjustments to occur.

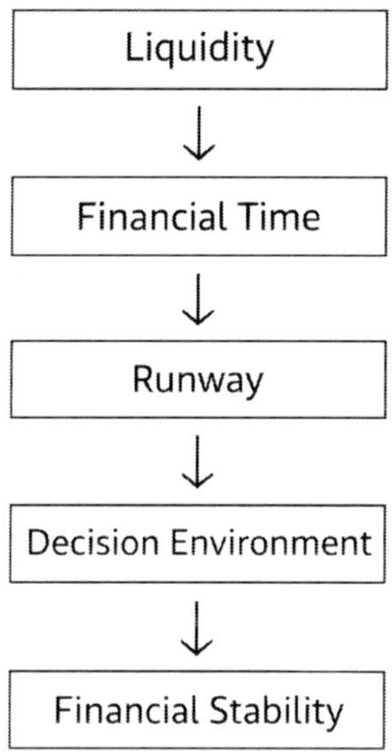

[Diagram 2 - Liquidity and Financial Time]

When a household holds sufficient liquidity, financial disturbances slow down. Essential obligations can still be met while solutions are evaluated. Decisions can be made sequentially rather than simultaneously. The system retains operational stability during the adjustment period.

Liquidity therefore functions as a shock absorber.

It does not prevent disturbances from occurring. Instead, it absorbs their immediate impact and distributes the adjustment process across time.

Without liquidity, disturbances move through the financial structure at full speed. Income disruptions immediately threaten essential obligations.

Bills approach faster than solutions can be implemented. The system enters reactive mode.

With liquidity, disturbances move more slowly. The household gains the ability to observe conditions, assess alternatives, and respond deliberately.

This difference in reaction time fundamentally changes the stability of the financial system.

Households with extended financial runway operate with more decision time. They have the capacity to wait for better options, negotiate obligations, or restructure expenses gradually.

Households with minimal runway operate within narrow decision windows. Options must be selected quickly because the financial structure cannot continue operating without immediate action.

Liquidity therefore defines the time horizon available for problem solving.

The longer the runway, the more time the household possesses to stabilize its financial structure when uncertainty appears.

The shorter the runway, the faster financial systems are forced into crisis decisions.

Understanding this relationship between liquidity and time is essential for understanding financial stability itself.

In household finance, stability is rarely determined by the absence of problems.

It is determined by the amount of time available to solve them.

Financial systems operate through decisions. Every payment, expense adjustment, borrowing action, or restructuring of obligations requires a choice. Under stable conditions, these decisions occur gradually and with sufficient time for evaluation.

Liquidity makes this gradual pace possible.

When liquidity is present, households have the ability to observe conditions before acting. Options can be compared. Consequences can be considered. Decisions can be delayed long enough for better information to emerge.

This process preserves decision quality.

However, when liquidity disappears, the timing of decisions changes dramatically.

Without liquidity, the household loses the ability to extend time between disturbance and response. Obligations continue to arrive on schedule even when income becomes uncertain. Bills must be paid immediately. Deadlines approach rapidly.

As a result, the financial system enters a state that can be described as decision compression.

Decision compression occurs when the available time for evaluating options collapses. Choices that would normally be considered over weeks or months must now be made within days or even hours.

This compression changes the nature of financial decision-making.

Under compressed conditions, households are not selecting the best available option. They are selecting the fastest option capable of resolving immediate pressure.

Speed becomes more important than quality.

For example, a household experiencing a temporary income interruption may normally choose between multiple adjustments: reducing discretionary spending, negotiating payment schedules, drawing from savings, or temporarily restructuring obligations.

If liquidity is available, these options can be evaluated calmly. The household can select the approach that minimizes long-term disruption.

If liquidity is absent, the evaluation process disappears. The household must immediately produce funds to meet obligations. Borrowing becomes the fastest available response, even if it creates new obligations that will persist long after the original disturbance has passed.

The decision is not necessarily irrational. It is a product of time scarcity.

Decision compression therefore transforms how financial systems behave. As reaction time disappears, financial structures become reactive rather than deliberate. The system begins to prioritize immediate survival rather than long-term stability.

This pattern explains why liquidity shortages often lead to cascading financial problems.

The initial disturbance may be relatively small — a temporary expense increase or a brief income disruption. However, because the household lacks reaction time, the response to that disturbance introduces new structural pressure.

Borrowing increases fixed obligations. Asset sales reduce future resilience. Payment delays create additional penalties.

Each compressed decision attempts to resolve immediate pressure, but the cumulative effect weakens the system further.

In contrast, households with sufficient liquidity experience disturbances very differently.

Because they possess reaction time, they can slow the decision process. Options can be evaluated sequentially rather than simultaneously. Temporary disturbances can be absorbed without restructuring the entire financial system.

Liquidity therefore protects decision quality by preserving financial time.

It prevents the compression of financial choices and allows households to maintain deliberate control over their financial structure.

Without liquidity, the timing of decisions collapses.

And when financial decisions must occur faster than they can be properly evaluated, stability becomes increasingly difficult to maintain.

Financial stability is often attributed to income level, budgeting discipline, or investment performance. These elements certainly influence household finance, but they do not fully explain why some financial systems remain stable during disruption while others quickly destabilize.

The underlying mechanism is simpler and more structural.

Financial stability is governed by a chain of relationships that begins with uncertainty.

Income uncertainty is an unavoidable feature of household finance. Employment conditions change, economic environments shift, businesses fluctuate, and unexpected events interrupt normal financial flows. Even highly stable income sources occasionally experience disruption.

Because uncertainty cannot be eliminated, financial systems must be structured to absorb it.

The first component of that structure is liquidity.

Liquidity determines reaction time.

When income becomes uncertain or temporarily interrupted, liquidity allows a household to continue operating while adjustments are made. Essential expenses can still be paid. Obligations remain satisfied. The household maintains operational continuity while evaluating possible responses.

The length of this reaction time is determined by financial runway.

Financial runway measures how long the household can sustain its existing structure without incoming income. The longer the runway, the more time the household possesses to respond carefully to financial disturbances.

Reaction time then determines decision quality.

When households possess sufficient reaction time, decisions can be evaluated deliberately. Alternatives can be compared. Trade-offs can be considered. Adjustments can be implemented gradually rather than abruptly.

Decision-making remains controlled and analytical.

When reaction time disappears, decision quality deteriorates. Households must respond immediately to financial pressure. The objective becomes resolving the next obligation rather than stabilizing the entire system.

In this environment, decisions are driven by urgency rather than evaluation.

Over time, the quality of these decisions determines the stability of the financial structure.

High-quality decisions maintain structural balance. Expenses are adjusted carefully. Obligations remain manageable. Temporary disturbances are absorbed without long-term damage.

Low-quality decisions gradually destabilize the system. Borrowing accumulates, obligations increase, and financial flexibility disappears. Each new disturbance becomes harder to manage than the last.

The governing chain can therefore be summarized clearly:

Income uncertainty

↓

Liquidity determines reaction time

↓

Reaction time determines decision quality

↓

Decision quality determines stability

This sequence explains why households with similar incomes can experience very different financial outcomes.

The difference is not necessarily how much money they earn. The difference is how much time their financial structure can produce when uncertainty appears.

Liquidity creates that time. Financial runway measures it.

Understanding this relationship is the central purpose of this book.

Household financial systems do not become stable simply because income is high or expenses are controlled. They become stable when sufficient financial time exists to manage uncertainty without forcing compressed decisions.

The chapters that follow examine how households construct this time within their financial structures.

They will explore how financial runway can be measured and how different financial choices influence the length and resilience of that runway.

Ultimately, the question guiding this book is straightforward:

If financial stability depends on time, the next question becomes clear: how do households build, measure, and protect financial runway?

Liquidity vs Wealth

Wealth and stability are often treated as interchangeable concepts in household finance. When a household accumulates assets, observers frequently assume that financial security has been achieved. Net worth becomes the shorthand measure of strength. A household with significant assets appears resilient, while a household with few assets appears fragile.

This interpretation reflects how financial value is commonly understood. Assets represent accumulated resources, and higher levels of accumulated resources seem to imply greater protection against uncertainty.

Yet financial stability is not determined solely by the amount of value a household possesses.

Stability depends on whether those resources can provide operational time when disruption occurs. A household may hold substantial financial value while still lacking the liquidity required to absorb disturbances. In such cases, wealth exists on paper but does not translate into the financial time necessary to maintain stability.

Understanding the difference between wealth and liquidity is therefore essential for analyzing how financial systems actually behave under pressure.

In most financial discussions, wealth is treated as the ultimate indicator of financial strength. The logic appears straightforward. A household that has accumulated assets possesses resources that can be used when necessary.

If unexpected expenses arise or income becomes uncertain, those assets appear to provide protection.

For this reason, net worth is widely used as a benchmark for financial progress. Households track the value of their homes, investment portfolios, retirement accounts, and savings balances. As these assets grow, financial security is assumed to increase.

This assumption reflects a basic principle: accumulated resources expand a household's capacity to absorb shocks.

However, the relationship between wealth and stability is more complex than it initially appears.

Wealth measures total financial value. Stability, by contrast, depends on the timing of access to that value. When disturbances occur, the critical question is not how much value exists in total but how quickly that value can be mobilized.

Assets grow over time through savings, appreciation, and investment returns. Because this growth process unfolds slowly, it is easy to assume accumulated value automatically translates into operational resilience.

Yet financial disturbances do not always unfold slowly.

Income interruptions, unexpected expenses, or economic disruptions can appear suddenly. When these events occur, the financial system must respond immediately in order to maintain operational continuity. Bills continue to arrive on schedule, essential expenses remain unavoidable, and obligations must still be met.

At that moment, the structure of the household's assets becomes critical.

If the household's resources exist primarily in forms that cannot easily be accessed, the system may possess significant wealth while still lacking the ability to respond quickly. The value exists, but it cannot immediately produce financial time.

This disconnect explains why households with substantial net worth sometimes experience financial pressure during relatively short disruptions.

A household may own a valuable home, maintain large retirement accounts, or hold significant investments while still struggling to meet obligations during an income interruption. The assets remain intact, but they do not provide the immediate flexibility required to stabilize the system.

From a wealth perspective, the household appears strong.

From an operational perspective, the household lacks liquidity.

This difference highlights an important structural distinction. Wealth measures accumulated value, while stability depends on usable liquidity. Wealth can exist in forms that are structurally slow to access, constrained by rules, or dependent on external conditions.

When disturbances occur, those constraints determine whether assets can function as stabilizing resources.

Because wealth is visible and easily measured, it often becomes the dominant indicator of financial strength. Yet this measurement obscures an important question: whether the household's financial structure can produce time when uncertainty appears.

Stability requires time. Wealth does not automatically produce it.

Understanding this difference is essential for analyzing how household financial systems behave during disruption.

Financial value and liquidity are often discussed together, but they represent distinct properties within a financial system.

Value refers to the economic worth of an asset. Homes, investment portfolios, retirement accounts, and other holdings represent stores of value that contribute to a household's net worth. These assets may appreciate over time, increasing the total financial resources available to the household.

Liquidity, by contrast, refers to immediate accessibility.

An asset is liquid if it can be converted into usable funds quickly, reliably, and without substantial disruption to the financial system. Liquidity therefore determines how easily financial value can be transformed into operational resources.

This distinction becomes particularly important during financial disturbances.

When income becomes uncertain or expenses increase unexpectedly, households must continue meeting obligations while they adjust their financial structure. The system requires resources that can be used immediately in order to maintain continuity.

Assets that cannot be accessed quickly provide limited assistance during this period.

For example, a household may own a home with significant equity. From a net worth perspective, this equity represents substantial financial value. However, accessing that value requires a series of steps that may involve refinancing, selling the property, or securing external financing.

Each of these processes requires time, coordination, and favorable external conditions.

During short-term disruption, these conditions may not exist. The household may need funds within days or weeks in order to maintain operational stability. Home equity, while valuable, may not be able to provide liquidity within that timeframe.

Similar dynamics appear in other asset categories.

Retirement accounts often represent large portions of household wealth, but they are designed primarily for long-term accumulation. Withdrawals may be restricted by tax rules, penalties, or administrative delays. As a result, these assets function as long-term stores of value rather than immediate sources of liquidity.

Investment portfolios also contain varying levels of liquidity depending on how they are structured. Some securities can be sold quickly, but doing so may depend on market conditions or may introduce tax consequences that alter the household's financial position.

These characteristics illustrate the structural difference between value and liquidity.

An asset can possess substantial value while remaining operationally inaccessible during periods of short-term disruption. The value exists within the financial system, but it cannot easily be converted into the time needed to stabilize the system.

Liquidity therefore functions as the bridge between value and time.

Only when financial value can be accessed quickly does it become capable of producing the reaction time necessary to absorb disturbances. Without this accessibility, wealth remains largely static during periods when the financial system requires immediate flexibility.

This distinction explains why households with large asset bases can still encounter liquidity pressure during disruptions.

The system possesses value but lacks the ability to convert it into usable financial time.

Understanding this difference between value and liquidity is essential for evaluating the stability of a household financial structure.

Certain assets strengthen a household's net worth while simultaneously reducing the amount of usable liquidity available during disruption. These situations can be described as household liquidity traps.

A household liquidity trap occurs when financial value accumulates in forms that are difficult to access quickly. The household's balance sheet appears stronger because total assets increase, yet the operational flexibility of the financial system may not improve.

In some cases, it may even decline.

One of the most common examples is residential property. Home ownership often represents the largest component of household wealth. As property values rise and mortgage balances decline, home equity increases. From a net worth perspective, this growth appears to strengthen financial security.

However, home equity is structurally illiquid.

Accessing that equity typically requires refinancing, obtaining a home equity loan, or selling the property. Each option involves time, administrative processes, and external approval. During periods of financial disruption, these processes may not align with the household's immediate liquidity needs.

As a result, large amounts of financial value remain embedded within the property while the household simultaneously faces short-term liquidity pressure.

Retirement accounts represent another common liquidity trap.

These accounts are designed to accumulate assets over long time horizons. Contribution incentives, tax advantages, and withdrawal restrictions encourage households to preserve these funds until retirement. While this structure supports long-term financial planning, it also means that the assets are not easily available during short-term disruptions.

Early withdrawals may involve penalties or tax consequences that significantly reduce the effective value of the funds. Administrative delays may also limit the speed at which withdrawals can occur.

The result is a concentration of financial value that cannot easily be converted into immediate liquidity.

Concentrated investments can produce similar dynamics.

A household may hold a large position in a particular investment or business asset. While the asset may contribute substantially to net worth, its liquidity may depend on market conditions, transaction processes, or buyer availability. Selling the asset quickly may require accepting unfavorable terms or substantial price reductions.

In each of these examples, financial value accumulates while operational liquidity remains limited.

This imbalance creates a structural vulnerability within the financial system. The household appears financially strong because net worth is high, but the system lacks the liquidity required to produce financial time during disruption.

Liquidity traps therefore distort the relationship between wealth and stability.

They increase total financial value while reducing the household's ability to respond quickly to disturbances. The balance sheet grows stronger on paper while the operational resilience of the system remains constrained.

Recognizing these traps is important because they reveal that asset accumulation alone does not guarantee stability.

The composition of assets — not simply their total value — determines how effectively a household can convert wealth into financial time.

If wealth does not automatically produce stability, then the question becomes what actually determines the resilience of a household financial system.

The answer returns to the concept introduced earlier in the book: financial time.

Financial time represents the duration a household can continue operating while responding to disruption. It measures the distance between the appearance of financial pressure and the point at which the system can no longer maintain its obligations.

This distance is the household's stability margin.

When financial time is abundant, disturbances unfold gradually. Households can observe conditions, evaluate alternatives, and implement adjustments in a controlled manner. Decisions occur sequentially rather than simultaneously, and the system retains structural balance.

When financial time is limited, disturbances accelerate. Obligations approach rapidly, and the household must respond immediately. Decisions are made under pressure because the financial system cannot continue operating without quick intervention.

The difference between these conditions determines whether disruption becomes manageable or destabilizing.

Liquidity is the mechanism that produces financial time.

Liquid resources allow households to continue meeting obligations while solutions are developed. The presence of liquidity slows the propagation of financial shocks, providing space for deliberate decision-making and structural adjustment.

Without liquidity, financial value cannot easily translate into operational time.

Assets may exist within the system, but they cannot be mobilized quickly enough to absorb short-term disturbances. The financial structure therefore behaves as though those resources are temporarily unavailable.

This dynamic explains why households with significant wealth sometimes experience instability during relatively small disruptions.

The assets that contribute to net worth do not necessarily produce the financial time required to maintain stability.

From a systems perspective, the critical variable is therefore not total wealth but usable liquidity that can produce financial time.

Wealth represents accumulated financial capacity. Liquidity determines whether that capacity can be deployed when the system requires it.

When liquidity is sufficient, financial disturbances can be absorbed without forcing immediate structural change. The system continues operating while adjustments are evaluated and implemented.

When liquidity is insufficient, disturbances propagate rapidly through the financial structure. The household must respond immediately, often introducing new obligations that persist beyond the original disruption.

Stability therefore emerges not from the size of the balance sheet but from the amount of financial time the system can produce.

The stability margin expands when liquidity creates sufficient reaction time. It contracts when financial value becomes trapped in assets that cannot easily be accessed.

Understanding this distinction allows household financial systems to be evaluated more accurately.

Net worth describes how much value exists within the system. Liquidity determines whether that value can generate the financial time required to maintain stability.

In practice, it is financial time — not total wealth — that ultimately determines whether households remain stable when uncertainty appears.

The Concept of Financial Runway

Households accumulate savings, build assets, and increase income in order to strengthen their financial position. These actions increase the amount of financial value contained within the household system.

However, value alone does not fully explain stability.

The stability of a financial system depends on how long the system can continue operating when disruption occurs. Income interruptions, unexpected expenses, and economic changes introduce uncertainty into household finances. When these disturbances appear, the system must continue functioning while adjustments are made.

The key variable becomes time.

A household that can continue operating for several months without incoming income experiences disruption differently than a household that can operate only for a few weeks. In the first case, the household has space to evaluate options and adjust its financial structure gradually. In the second case, the household must respond immediately in order to maintain operational continuity.

This difference in reaction time is captured in the concept of financial runway.

Financial runway measures the length of time a household can sustain its existing financial structure when income becomes uncertain or temporarily stops. It converts liquidity into operational time within the household financial system.

Understanding runway allows financial stability to be examined in temporal terms rather than simply in terms of accumulated resources. Instead of asking how much money a household possesses, the more relevant question becomes how long the household can continue operating if income is disrupted.

The answer to that question reveals the amount of financial time the system contains.

Financial runway is a measure of financial time.

It represents the amount of financial time a household can continue meeting essential expenses using existing liquid resources when income becomes uncertain or temporarily stops. In practical terms, runway measures how long the financial system can remain functional before structural adjustments become unavoidable.

This concept reframes liquidity in temporal terms.

Liquidity represents accessible financial resources. Runway represents the time those resources can sustain the financial system. When liquidity is translated into time, the household gains a clearer understanding of how its financial structure behaves during disruption.

The relationship can be expressed through a simple structural equation:

Runway = Liquidity ÷ Burn Rate

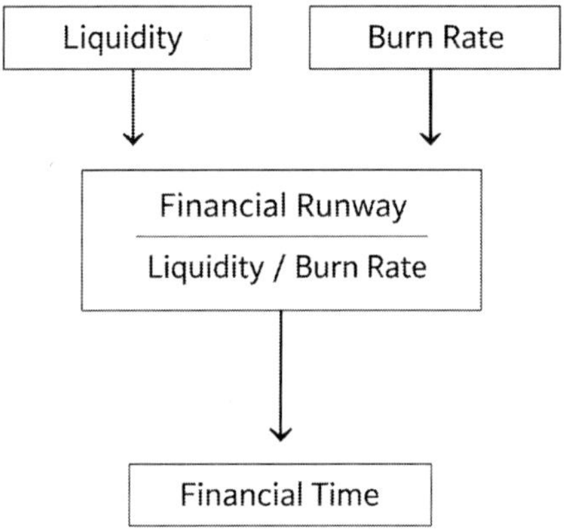

[Diagram 3 - Financial Runway Structure]

In this equation, liquidity represents the financial resources that can be accessed immediately or within a short time frame. These resources include cash balances, savings accounts, and other funds that can be used without significant delay.

Burn rate represents the speed at which these resources are consumed by essential ongoing expenses.

Together, these two variables determine how long the household can continue operating without incoming income.

To illustrate the concept, consider a simple example.

A household possesses $12,000 in accessible liquidity.
Its monthly expenses total $3,000.

Using the runway equation:

$12,000 liquidity

÷ $3,000 monthly burn rate

Runway = 4 months

This means the household can continue meeting its essential expenses for approximately four months without incoming income.

Rather than viewing savings as a static amount of money, runway reveals how that amount translates into time.

This translation matters because disturbances occur across time.

Income interruptions may last weeks or months. Employment transitions may require time to resolve. Unexpected expenses may create temporary imbalances that must be absorbed before the system returns to equilibrium.

Financial runway determines whether the household can remain operational during these periods.

When runway is long, the financial system has space to adjust gradually. The household can evaluate options, reorganize expenses, or search for new income without immediate pressure.

When runway is short, disturbances quickly reach the point where obligations cannot be met. The household must respond immediately, often before full information about the situation is available.

Runway therefore functions as a measure of financial time within the system.

It measures the stability margin between the onset of disruption and the moment when the system can no longer continue operating without structural change.

Understanding this buffer allows households to evaluate their financial stability more accurately. Rather than focusing solely on how much liquidity exists, runway reveals how long that liquidity can sustain the system under stress.

The concept of runway therefore converts liquidity into financial time.

If liquidity determines how many resources are available, burn rate determines how quickly those resources are consumed.

Burn rate refers to the speed at which a household's financial system uses liquid resources when income is absent or uncertain. It is effectively the pace at which expenses draw down available liquidity.

Understanding burn rate is essential because it defines the time horizon that liquidity can produce.

Two households with identical liquidity may experience very different financial runways depending on the rate at which their resources are consumed.

Consider the following example.

Household A holds $15,000 in liquid resources.

Household B also holds $15,000 in liquid resources.

At first glance, the two households appear to possess identical financial capacity.

However, their expense structures differ.

Household A has monthly expenses of $3,000.

$15,000 liquidity

÷ $3,000 burn rate

Runway = 5 months

Household B has monthly expenses of $5,000.

$15,000 liquidity

÷ $5,000 burn rate

Runway = 3 months

Even though both households hold the same amount of liquidity, their financial runway differs by two months.

The difference arises entirely from burn rate.

Burn rate therefore represents the operational speed of the financial system. It reflects the structure of expenses that must be sustained in order for the household to maintain normal operations.

These expenses typically include housing costs, utilities, food, insurance, transportation, and other recurring obligations. Because many of these costs are fixed or semi-fixed, the burn rate of a household often remains relatively stable over short periods of time.

This stability allows burn rate to function as a reliable measure of how quickly liquidity will be consumed during disruption.

When income stops or becomes uncertain, burn rate determines how rapidly the household's liquidity buffer declines. A higher burn rate shortens runway because resources are consumed more quickly. A lower burn rate extends runway because resources last longer.

Importantly, burn rate does not necessarily reflect discretionary spending alone. Many components of household burn rate are structural obligations that cannot easily be adjusted in the short term.

Housing payments, insurance premiums, and other contractual expenses continue regardless of whether income is temporarily disrupted. As a result, burn rate reflects the operational requirements of the financial system rather than simply lifestyle preferences.

Understanding burn rate therefore provides insight into how sensitive a household's financial runway is to disruption.

A system with a high burn rate requires larger liquidity reserves in order to maintain the same amount of financial time. A system with a lower burn rate can sustain longer operational periods using the same level of liquidity.

In this way, burn rate functions as the denominator of the runway equation.

It determines how efficiently liquidity is converted into financial time.

Because runway translates liquidity into financial time, measuring runway provides a direct way to evaluate the resilience of a household financial system.

The process for measuring runway is conceptually simple. Two inputs are required: the amount of accessible liquidity and the household's burn rate.

Liquidity refers to financial resources that can be accessed quickly without requiring asset sales, borrowing, or complex administrative processes. These resources typically include checking balances, savings accounts, and other funds that are immediately available for operational use.

Burn rate represents the monthly level of expenses that must be sustained to maintain normal household operations.

Once these two values are identified, runway can be calculated using the equation introduced earlier:

Runway = Liquidity ÷ Burn Rate

This calculation converts the household's available liquidity into a time measurement.

Consider a second illustration.

A household possesses $18,000 in accessible liquidity.

Its monthly burn rate is $4,500.

Applying the runway equation:

$18,000 liquidity

÷ $4,500 burn rate

Runway = 4 months

This result indicates that the household can continue meeting its expenses for four months if income becomes temporarily unavailable.

Rather than viewing liquidity as an abstract financial cushion, runway expresses the cushion in terms of time.

This time horizon determines how the household experiences financial disruption.

If an income interruption lasts one month, a four-month runway allows the system to absorb the disturbance without requiring structural changes. If the interruption extends beyond four months, adjustments to expenses or obligations may become necessary.

Runway therefore functions as an early indicator of financial pressure.

Short runway signals that disturbances will quickly force the household into urgent decision-making. Long runway signals that the system can tolerate uncertainty for extended periods without destabilizing.

The measurement also reveals how small changes in either liquidity or burn rate can alter the time horizon of the system.

For example:

Liquidity: $10,000

Burn Rate: $2,500

Runway: 4 months

If the burn rate increases to $3,000 while liquidity remains unchanged:

Liquidity: $10,000

Burn Rate: $3,000/month

Runway: ≈ 3.3 months

The increase in expenses shortens the household's operational horizon even though liquidity has not changed.

Similarly, increasing liquidity while burn rate remains constant lengthens runway and expands the amount of time available for decision-making.

Because of this sensitivity, runway provides a useful way to observe how structural changes within the household financial system affect stability.

It translates the balance between resources and expenses into a single temporal measurement that reflects how the system will behave when disruption occurs.

Liquidity alone represents stored financial capacity.

Runway converts that capacity into financial time.

This transformation makes runway such a powerful concept within household finance. When liquidity is expressed as time rather than as dollars, the stability of the financial system becomes easier to understand.

Financial disturbances unfold across time. Income interruptions may last several weeks or several months. Employment transitions may require time to resolve. Unexpected expenses may create temporary imbalances that must be absorbed before equilibrium is restored.

Runway determines whether the household can remain stable during these periods.

When runway is long, disturbances unfold slowly. The household possesses the ability to observe conditions, evaluate options, and implement adjustments deliberately. Decisions occur sequentially rather than simultaneously.

This deliberate pace preserves decision quality.

When runway is short, disturbances propagate quickly. Obligations approach rapidly, and the household must respond before the situation is fully understood. Decisions become reactive because the system lacks the time required for careful evaluation.

In this way, runway defines the decision environment of the financial system.

It determines whether financial decisions occur in a stable environment or under urgency.

This distinction directly influences the stability margin of the household financial system.

The stability margin represents the distance between the current financial structure and the point at which the system can no longer meet its obligations. Runway expands this margin by providing time for disturbances to be absorbed.

The longer the runway, the greater the stability margin.

When runway is extended, disturbances are less likely to force immediate structural change. The system can tolerate uncertainty while maintaining operational continuity.

When runway is limited, the stability margin narrows. Even small disruptions can quickly move the system toward instability because the available reaction time is short.

Runway therefore functions as the temporal foundation of household financial stability.

It does not eliminate financial disturbances, nor does it guarantee that disruptions will be painless. Instead, it determines how much time the household possesses to manage those disruptions without destabilizing the system.

This time governs the quality of financial decisions and the resilience of the overall structure.

Understanding financial runway allows households to evaluate their financial position in operational terms rather than simply in terms of accumulated resources.

The central question becomes not how much money exists within the system, but how long the system can continue operating when uncertainty appears.

Runway provides the measure.

Decision Compression Under Constraint

Financial systems typically operate through a sequence of decisions made over time. Income is allocated to expenses, obligations are scheduled according to predictable timelines, and adjustments occur gradually as circumstances change. Under stable conditions, households evaluate options, compare alternatives, and make financial choices with sufficient time for analysis.

Payments occur automatically, income arrives on schedule, and the financial structure continues functioning without requiring frequent intervention. The system appears steady because decisions occur within an environment where time is available.

However, this stability depends on the presence of financial time.

When liquidity declines and financial runway becomes short, the timing of financial decisions changes. Obligations continue to arrive according to fixed schedules while the resources required to meet those obligations begin to diminish. As the distance between obligations and available resources narrows, the amount of time available for evaluating financial choices begins to collapse.

This condition can be described as decision compression.

Decision compression occurs when the time available to evaluate financial options disappears. Under these circumstances, households must make choices quickly in order to maintain operational continuity.

Decisions that might normally unfold across weeks or months must now occur within days or even hours.

When financial systems enter this compressed decision environment, the nature of financial choices changes. Decisions are no longer structured around long-term stability. Instead, they are structured around immediate survival.

Understanding how decision compression emerges — and how it alters the behavior of household financial systems — is essential for understanding the role financial runway plays in maintaining stability.

Financial time represents the interval between the appearance of financial pressure and the moment when obligations can no longer be met without structural change. This interval allows households to evaluate options and adjust their financial systems deliberately.

When financial runway is long, this interval provides time between disturbance and response.

Income interruptions, unexpected expenses, or other disruptions may alter the financial structure temporarily, but the presence of liquidity allows the system to continue operating while adjustments are considered. The household retains control over the timing of its decisions.

However, when runway becomes short, this interval begins to collapse.

Liquidity declines while expenses remain constant. Obligations continue to arrive according to fixed schedules, but the resources required to meet those obligations are no longer sufficient to sustain the system for extended periods. The distance between available liquidity and upcoming expenses narrows rapidly.

As this distance shrinks, financial time disappears.

Each passing week or month reduces the remaining operational horizon. Instead of having months to evaluate options, the household may have only weeks.

In some cases, it may shrink to days.

At this stage, the household's financial structure begins to operate under immediate pressure. The system can no longer wait for conditions to improve or for better information to become available. Decisions must be made quickly because obligations are approaching faster than solutions can be implemented.

The disappearance of financial time fundamentally changes the environment in which financial decisions occur.

Under stable conditions, households make decisions within a broad time horizon. Expenses can be adjusted gradually, obligations renegotiated, and alternative income sources explored. Each decision occurs within a process that allows careful evaluation.

When financial time disappears, this process collapses.

The household must respond immediately to maintain operational continuity. Instead of evaluating the full range of available options, the household must select whichever option resolves the most immediate pressure.

The difference between these environments is not simply psychological. It is structural.

Financial systems require time in order to function deliberately. Without time, the system shifts into a reactive mode where decisions are driven primarily by urgency.

This shift marks the beginning of decision compression.

The financial system still operates, but the timing of its decisions has changed dramatically. Instead of operating within a controlled sequence of evaluations and adjustments, the system is now forced to respond to events as they occur.

As runway continues to shorten, this reactive environment intensifies. Each decision must be made more quickly than the last because the system lacks the time required for careful evaluation.

In this way, the disappearance of financial time transforms the decision environment of the household.

It replaces deliberate financial management with urgent response.

Decision compression emerges when the timing of financial obligations exceeds the household's available reaction time. Liquidity declines while expenses remain constant, forcing the household to resolve financial pressure quickly.

Under these conditions, the mechanics of financial decision-making change in several important ways.

First, the range of available options narrows.

When financial time is abundant, households can consider multiple approaches to resolving a disturbance. They may reorganize expenses gradually, negotiate payment schedules, adjust discretionary spending, or seek additional income. Because obligations are not immediately pressing, each option can be evaluated carefully.

When financial time disappears, this evaluation process becomes impossible.

The household cannot wait long enough to compare alternatives. Instead, it must select whichever option provides the fastest relief from immediate financial pressure. The objective shifts from selecting the best solution to selecting the quickest solution.

Second, the sequence of financial decisions accelerates.

Under normal conditions, financial adjustments occur gradually. Households make one decision, observe the results, and then determine whether additional changes are necessary. This sequential process allows the financial structure to stabilize after each adjustment.

In a compressed environment, decisions occur in rapid succession.

Multiple financial pressures may appear simultaneously as obligations approach and liquidity declines. Because each obligation requires immediate attention, the household must resolve several decisions at once rather than sequentially.

Third, uncertainty increases.

When decisions must be made quickly, households often lack complete information about the consequences of each option. Income prospects may be uncertain, expenses may fluctuate, and the duration of the disturbance may remain unclear.

Under stable conditions, households can wait for additional information before acting. Under compressed conditions, waiting is no longer possible.

Decisions must be made despite incomplete information because obligations cannot be postponed.

Finally, the objective of financial decision-making changes.

When financial time is available, decisions can be optimized for long-term stability. Households can consider how each choice affects their financial structure over months or years.

When financial time disappears, the objective becomes immediate survival.

The household must ensure that the next obligation can be met, even if the solution introduces new constraints or obligations in the future. The focus shifts from optimizing the system to preserving its short-term operation.

These changes define the mechanics of decision compression.

The financial system continues to function, but its decision process is no longer governed by deliberate evaluation. Instead, it is governed by the urgency of approaching obligations.

The shorter the financial runway becomes, the more compressed the decision environment grows.

Understanding this mechanism explains why liquidity plays such an important role in household financial stability. Liquidity extends the time available for decision-making, preventing the compression of financial choices.

Without liquidity, the system must respond to disturbances faster than those disturbances can be evaluated.

Decision compression rarely affects a single financial choice in isolation. Instead, it often produces a sequence of decisions that interact with one another, creating cascading pressure within the financial system.

This cascade begins with the initial disturbance that reduces financial runway.

An income interruption, unexpected expense, or other financial shock reduces the household's liquidity. As liquidity declines, the available time for responding to financial pressure shrinks. Obligations continue to arrive while the household's ability to absorb them diminishes.

Once the system enters a compressed decision environment, each response to financial pressure can introduce additional constraints.

For example, a household facing an immediate payment obligation may choose to borrow funds in order to maintain operational continuity. Borrowing provides rapid access to liquidity and therefore resolves the immediate pressure.

However, borrowing also introduces new obligations.

Future payments must now include the repayment of borrowed funds along with interest or fees. These new obligations increase the household's burn rate, which reduces the amount of runway available for responding to future disturbances.

Similarly, households may delay certain payments in order to meet more urgent obligations. While this strategy may preserve liquidity temporarily, it can introduce penalties, fees, or service disruptions that increase financial pressure later.

Another common response involves selling assets in order to generate liquidity. In some cases, assets must be sold quickly to meet immediate obligations. Rapid sales may occur under unfavorable conditions, reducing the effective value of the assets being liquidated.

Each of these responses resolves an immediate problem but introduces new structural pressures.

As a result, the system becomes increasingly fragile. Future disturbances require faster responses because the household's stability margin has narrowed.

This dynamic explains why financial instability often accelerates once liquidity disappears.

The initial disturbance may be relatively small. However, because the household lacks financial time, the responses required to maintain operational continuity gradually weaken the financial structure.

New obligations accumulate, liquidity buffers shrink, and the system becomes increasingly sensitive to additional disturbances.

The result is a cascade of financial pressure.

Each compressed decision attempts to resolve the immediate problem, but the cumulative effect increases the system's vulnerability. Over time, the household may find itself operating in a permanent state of decision compression, where every financial obligation requires urgent attention.

This pattern illustrates how the absence of liquidity can transform a temporary disturbance into a sustained period of financial instability.

The system does not fail immediately. Instead, it becomes trapped in a sequence of reactive decisions that gradually erode the stability margin of the household financial structure.

If decision compression destabilizes household financial systems, the opposite condition — available financial time — preserves stability.

Available financial time exists when financial runway provides sufficient time for households to evaluate financial options deliberately. Instead of responding immediately to each disturbance, the household can observe conditions, gather information, and implement adjustments gradually.

This deliberate decision environment protects the stability margin of the financial system.

When runway is long, disturbances unfold slowly relative to the household's ability to respond. Liquidity absorbs the immediate effects of disruption, allowing the system to continue operating while solutions are evaluated.

In this environment, financial decisions occur sequentially rather than simultaneously.

A household experiencing an income interruption, for example, can first evaluate the expected duration of the disruption. It can then adjust discretionary spending, reorganize obligations, or seek alternative income sources. Each decision occurs within a controlled sequence rather than under immediate pressure.

Because decisions occur with sufficient time for evaluation, the solutions chosen are more likely to preserve the long-term stability of the financial structure.

Runway does not eliminate uncertainty or prevent financial disturbances from occurring. Instead, it provides the time required to respond intelligently when those disturbances appear.

In practical terms, this means that households with longer runway rarely experience the cascading financial pressure described earlier.

Even when disturbances occur, liquidity absorbs the initial shock and prevents the system from entering a compressed decision environment. The household remains in control of the timing and sequence of its financial choices.

This control expands the stability margin of the system.

The stability margin represents the distance between the household's current financial structure and the point at which obligations can no longer be sustained. Longer runway increases this distance by providing additional time for adjustments to occur.

Short runway reduces the margin and forces decisions to occur under pressure.

From a systems perspective, the stability of a household financial structure therefore depends on the availability of decision time.

Financial decisions require time for evaluation. When that time exists, households can respond to uncertainty deliberately and preserve the balance of the system.

When that time disappears, decisions become compressed, and stability becomes increasingly difficult to maintain.

Financial runway protects against this compression by converting liquidity into financial time.

In doing so, it allows households to maintain control over the pace and quality of financial decisions — a condition that lies at the core of financial stability.

Liquidity Layers

Liquidity is often described in simple terms. In many discussions of household finance, liquidity is equated with cash or savings balances. When a household holds money in a checking account or maintains a savings reserve, that money is commonly treated as the household's liquidity.

This description captures only part of the picture.

In practice, liquidity exists in several forms within a household financial system. Some resources are immediately accessible and can be used at any moment. Others require small administrative steps before they can be accessed. Still others require time, coordination, or external transactions before they can provide usable funds.

These differences create a layered structure of liquidity.

Each layer represents a different level of accessibility and speed. Some resources provide immediate financial time, while others require a delay before they can contribute to the system's stability. When financial disturbances occur, these layers activate at different speeds, absorbing pressure in stages.

Understanding liquidity as a layered system helps explain why some households maintain stability during disruption while others experience rapid financial pressure.

The strength of a household's financial structure depends not only on the total amount of liquidity it possesses, but also on how that liquidity is distributed across layers of accessibility.

A well-structured liquidity system allows disturbances to be absorbed across time.

A poorly structured system may contain significant financial value but lack the immediate resources needed to prevent financial pressure from spreading quickly through the household's obligations.

When liquidity is discussed in everyday financial conversations, it is often treated as a single pool of money. A household may be described as "having liquidity" if it maintains a certain amount of savings or keeps accessible liquidity in accessible accounts.

This simplified view suggests that liquidity functions as one unified resource within the financial system.

However, the structure of household finances is rarely that simple.

Different financial resources possess different levels of accessibility. Some funds can be used immediately without preparation or delay. Others require administrative processes, financial transactions, or external approval before they can become usable. These differences create variations in how quickly resources can respond to financial disturbances.

As a result, liquidity operates less like a single pool and more like a layered system of financial access.

Each layer represents a category of resources that can be mobilized at a particular speed.

At the most accessible level, liquidity exists in the form of immediately available funds. These resources can be used instantly to meet financial obligations as they arise. Because they require no delay or conversion process, they provide the fastest form of financial time.

At the next level, resources may still be highly accessible but require small steps before they can be used. Funds held in savings accounts, for example, may require transfers before they can be applied to expenses. While this process may take only minutes or hours, it still represents a distinct layer of liquidity within the financial system.

Beyond these layers lie resources that are technically accessible but require additional actions to convert into usable funds. Investments may need to be sold, accounts may need to be accessed through administrative processes, or financial arrangements may need to be executed before the funds become available.

Finally, some resources exist in forms that require significant time to convert into liquidity. These assets may hold substantial financial value, but the process of accessing that value may involve complex transactions, negotiations, or market conditions.

Because these layers differ in speed and accessibility, they behave differently during financial disturbances.

When a disturbance first appears, the most accessible resources absorb the initial pressure. If the disturbance continues, the system begins to draw upon deeper layers of liquidity that require additional steps to access.

Understanding liquidity as a layered structure clarifies why households with similar levels of total financial resources may experience very different stability outcomes. The difference often lies not in the amount of liquidity present, but in the accessibility of that liquidity.

Financial systems with well-structured liquidity layers can respond quickly to disturbances while preserving deeper resources for longer disruptions.

Systems that lack accessible liquidity may contain financial value but still struggle to respond effectively when obligations arrive faster than resources can be mobilized.

Because liquidity exists in different forms, household financial systems naturally develop a hierarchy of liquidity sources. Each layer within this hierarchy provides a different level of accessibility and response speed.

At the top of the hierarchy lies immediate cash.

Immediate cash represents the most accessible form of liquidity within the household system. These resources include funds held in checking accounts or other accounts designed for daily financial operations. Because these funds can be used instantly, they form the first line of financial response when obligations arise.

Immediate cash allows households to maintain day-to-day operational continuity. It supports the routine payment of bills, purchases, and other financial transactions that occur regularly within the household system.

The second layer consists of savings buffers.

Savings buffers are resources that remain highly accessible but are typically separated from daily spending accounts. These funds are often held in savings accounts or similar financial structures that allow relatively quick transfers into operational accounts.

Savings buffers serve as the first level of shock absorption. When unexpected expenses arise or when temporary income fluctuations occur, these resources can be deployed to maintain continuity without disrupting the household's broader financial structure.

As financial disturbances extend beyond the capacity of basic savings buffers, households begin to rely on deeper liquidity layers that require additional actions to access.

Beyond savings buffers lies the layer of accessible capital.

Accessible capital includes resources that can be converted into liquidity with moderate effort. Examples may include investment accounts that can be liquidated, financial instruments that can be redeemed, or other forms of financial capital that require a transaction process before funds become usable.

Although these resources are not immediately accessible in the same way as cash or savings, they can still contribute to the financial system's resilience during extended disturbances.

The final layer consists of convertible assets.

Convertible assets represent financial value that can eventually be transformed into liquidity but requires substantial time or structural change to do so. Real estate equity, ownership stakes in businesses, or other long-term assets may fall into this category.

These assets often represent significant portions of household wealth, but they are typically slow to access. Converting them into liquidity may involve selling property, restructuring financial arrangements, or engaging in complex transactions.

Because of these characteristics, convertible assets usually function as the deepest layer of liquidity within the household financial system.

Together, these layers form a hierarchy of financial accessibility.

Resources at the top of the hierarchy respond quickly but may be limited in quantity. Resources deeper in the hierarchy may contain larger amounts of value but require more time to access.

This structure reflects the trade-off between accessibility and accumulation within household finances.

Highly accessible funds tend to remain smaller because they are used regularly. Less accessible assets may accumulate more value over time because they are preserved for long-term purposes.

Understanding this hierarchy allows households to recognize how different forms of financial resources contribute to stability.

The effectiveness of the system depends not only on the presence of these layers but also on how they interact when disturbances occur.

The layered structure of liquidity allows household financial systems to absorb disturbances in stages. Each layer responds at a different speed, slowing the propagation of financial pressure in stages.

This process can be described as shock absorption.

Financial disturbances typically appear suddenly. An unexpected expense may arise, income may fluctuate, or external conditions may temporarily interrupt financial flows. When these events occur, the household system must respond immediately in order to maintain operational continuity.

The first response occurs within the most accessible liquidity layer.

Immediate cash absorbs the earliest impact of the disturbance. Because these funds are already positioned within the household's operational accounts, they can be used instantly to meet obligations. Payments continue to be made, and the disturbance does not immediately disrupt the household's financial operations.

If the disturbance persists beyond the capacity of immediate cash, the system begins to draw upon the next layer.

Savings buffers provide additional liquidity that can be transferred into operational accounts. These funds allow the household to maintain stability while evaluating the nature and duration of the disturbance.

During this stage, the system remains largely stable.

If the disruption extends further, the system may begin to activate deeper liquidity layers.

Accessible capital can be mobilized through transactions such as selling investments or redeeming financial instruments. Although this process may require several days or administrative steps, it provides additional financial time when disturbances extend beyond the capacity of reserve savings.

Finally, if disruption continues long enough, convertible assets may become relevant.

At this stage, the household may consider restructuring long-term assets in order to generate liquidity. Because these actions often involve complex transactions or structural changes, they are typically reserved for extended financial disturbances.

The layered response of liquidity therefore slows the spread of financial pressure.

Instead of allowing disturbances to immediately destabilize the entire financial system, the household absorbs pressure sequentially across multiple layers of liquidity. Each layer provides additional time for evaluation and adjustment.

This staged response is critical for maintaining financial stability.

Without liquidity layers, disturbances would propagate rapidly through the financial system. Obligations would immediately exceed available resources, forcing households into compressed decision environments.

Layered liquidity prevents this acceleration by distributing financial pressure across time.

Each layer acts as a temporary buffer, allowing the household to maintain control over the pace and sequence of financial adjustments.

Financial runway measures the amount of time a household can continue operating when income becomes uncertain. Liquidity layers determine how runway is structured.

Instead of existing as a single continuous resource, financial runway is often composed of multiple segments corresponding to different layers of liquidity.

Immediate cash may provide the first portion of financial time. Reserve savings extend that time further. Accessible capital and convertible assets provide additional layers that may become relevant during longer disruptions.

Together, these layers determine the full time horizon of the household financial system.

This layered runway structure increases the stability margin of the system.

When disturbances occur, the household does not immediately confront the limits of its financial capacity. Instead, each layer of liquidity provides additional time before deeper resources must be accessed.

The presence of multiple layers also allows households to respond to disruptions in stages.

Short disturbances may be absorbed entirely by the upper layers of liquidity. Immediate cash and savings buffers may provide sufficient financial time for the system to stabilize without requiring deeper adjustments.

Longer disruptions may require the activation of deeper layers, but these layers remain available because the earlier liquidity layers delayed the need to access them.

In this way, liquidity layers preserve the flexibility of the financial system.

By structuring liquidity across different levels of accessibility, households ensure that disturbances do not immediately force large structural changes. Instead, financial pressure is distributed across time and across resources.

When liquidity layers are present, households maintain control over the pace of their responses to disruption. Decisions can be evaluated sequentially rather than within a compressed decision environment.

Without layered liquidity, financial disturbances propagate rapidly through the system. Households may be forced to access deep assets prematurely or make compressed financial decisions because no intermediate liquidity layers exist.

The presence of liquidity layers therefore expands financial time.

Each layer extends the runway of the household system and strengthens its stability margin. The result is a financial structure capable of absorbing disturbances without losing operational control.

Understanding liquidity as a layered system provides a more accurate picture of how household finances function under stress.

Stability emerges not only from the total amount of liquidity present but from the way that liquidity is distributed across layers of accessibility.

These layers transform financial resources into structured financial time — a foundation for household financial stability.

The Structure of an Emergency Fund

Many households maintain some form of savings. Funds may accumulate in savings accounts, cash reserves, or other easily accessible financial holdings. These balances often serve multiple purposes simultaneously: they may support routine financial flexibility, future purchases, or general financial comfort.

However, within a household financial system, not all savings serve the same function.

Some funds operate as part of daily financial circulation, supporting routine expenses and short-term fluctuations in spending. Other resources are intended for long-term accumulation, such as retirement savings or investment assets. Between these two roles lies a distinct category of liquidity designed for a specific purpose: absorbing short-term financial disturbances.

This category is commonly referred to as an emergency fund.

An emergency fund functions as a dedicated liquidity layer within the household financial system. Its purpose is not to generate long-term financial growth or to finance routine spending. Instead, it exists to protect the system from entering instability when temporary disturbances occur.

Understanding this role requires recognizing that financial disturbances are a normal feature of household finances. Income flows fluctuate, expenses occasionally exceed expectations, and unexpected events introduce short-term volatility into otherwise stable financial structures.

When these disturbances occur, the presence or absence of a dedicated liquidity layer determines whether the system remains stable or enters a compressed decision environment.

The emergency fund therefore serves as a dedicated shock-absorption layer within the household's liquidity structure. By providing accessible resources that are reserved specifically for disturbances, it preserves the financial time required to maintain stability.

Household financial systems operate within environments that contain a constant degree of uncertainty. Income flows may appear predictable over long periods, but short-term fluctuations occur regularly. Working hours may change, employment transitions may occur, and business revenues may vary across seasons or economic conditions.

Expenses display similar variability.

Certain costs remain relatively stable, such as housing payments, insurance premiums, or contractual obligations. However, other expenses fluctuate unexpectedly. Health-related costs, repairs, transportation disruptions, and other unforeseen events introduce variability into household spending patterns.

These fluctuations represent normal characteristics of financial life rather than signs of structural failure.

In many cases, the financial disturbance itself is temporary. Income may be delayed but eventually restored. An unexpected expense may arise once and not recur for long periods. Repairs may occur sporadically but not continuously.

The disturbance itself may be limited in scope.

The difficulty arises when the household financial system lacks the buffers required to absorb these disturbances.

Without sufficient liquidity reserves, even temporary fluctuations can propagate quickly through the system. Income interruptions may arrive before expenses can be adjusted. Unexpected costs may exceed the resources immediately available to meet them. Obligations continue to arrive on schedule regardless of whether the household is prepared for the disturbance.

When this occurs, the system must respond immediately in order to maintain operational continuity.

Financial decisions that would normally be evaluated carefully must instead be made quickly. Resources must be located rapidly, obligations must be prioritized, and financial pressure increases as deadlines approach.

This environment represents the early stages of decision compression.

The underlying disturbance may not be severe, but the absence of a buffer forces the household to respond as as if it were urgent.

The key issue is therefore not the presence of disturbances but the system's capacity to absorb them.

Financial systems that possess adequate liquidity reserves treat disturbances as temporary fluctuations. These events may require adjustments, but they do not destabilize the entire structure.

Financial systems that lack liquidity reserves experience the same disturbances as destabilizing events because they have no mechanism to absorb the initial shock.

In this context, the role of an emergency fund becomes clear.

The emergency fund does not eliminate financial disturbances. Instead, it provides a dedicated mechanism for absorbing them without forcing the system into immediate structural change.

By acting as a shock-absorption layer, the emergency fund prevents temporary disturbances from escalating into broader financial instability.

Within the layered structure of household liquidity, the emergency fund occupies a distinct position.

While many financial resources contribute to a household's overall financial capacity, the emergency fund is specifically designed to address short-term disturbances. Its purpose is to provide immediately accessible liquidity that can absorb unexpected financial pressure without disrupting the broader financial system.

This function distinguishes emergency funds from several other forms of financial resources.

Daily operating cash, for example, supports routine financial activity. Funds held in checking accounts are used to pay regular bills, manage everyday purchases, and maintain the normal flow of financial transactions. Because these funds circulate continuously, they cannot reliably function as shock absorbers during financial disturbances.

Long-term savings serve a different purpose.

Households often accumulate savings for future expenditures such as education, housing transitions, or other anticipated financial events. These savings represent planned financial resources intended for specific goals rather than unplanned disruptions.

Although such savings may technically be accessible, using them to absorb financial disturbances may interfere with long-term financial objectives.

Investment assets operate at another level of the financial structure.

Investment accounts are typically designed to accumulate value over extended periods. Their purpose is to increase financial capacity through appreciation or income generation. While these assets contribute to overall wealth, they are not necessarily structured to provide immediate liquidity during short-term disruptions.

Selling investments may involve transaction delays, tax consequences, or unfavorable timing relative to market conditions.

The emergency fund differs from all of these resources because it is dedicated specifically to financial shock absorption.

Funds held within the emergency fund are not intended for routine spending, long-term accumulation, or planned expenditures. Instead, they remain reserved for unexpected disturbances that threaten the operational continuity of the household financial system.

This dedicated role provides an important structural benefit.

Because the emergency fund is not intertwined with other financial objectives, it can be deployed quickly when disturbances occur. The household does not need to reorganize its broader financial structure or compromise long-term plans in order to respond to short-term financial pressure.

The emergency fund therefore functions as a protective layer in the liquidity hierarchy.

It absorbs the initial impact of financial disturbances and prevents those disturbances from propagating immediately through the rest of the financial system.

In doing so, the emergency fund protects the household from entering a compressed decision environment where financial choices must be made rapidly under pressure.

Instead, it preserves the time necessary for deliberate evaluation and adjustment.

Financial runway measures the amount of financial time a household can continue operating when income becomes uncertain or temporarily stops. Liquidity buffers directly influence this time horizon.

An emergency fund therefore plays a central role in determining the amount of runway available in a household financial system.

When disturbances occur, the emergency fund provides the first extension of financial time beyond the household's daily operating resources. Instead of immediately confronting the limits of available cash flow, the system gains access to a dedicated reserve of liquidity.

This reserve extends the operational horizon of the financial system.

Consider a simple illustration.

A household maintains $3,000 in immediate operating cash for routine expenses. Its monthly burn rate is also $3,000.

Without additional buffers, the household's operational runway is approximately one month if income becomes uncertain.

Now consider the same household with an emergency fund of $9,000.

Operating cash: $3,000

Emergency fund: $9,000

Total accessible liquidity: $12,000

With a burn rate of $3,000 per month:

$12,000 liquidity

÷ $3,000 burn rate

Runway = 4 months

The presence of the emergency fund expands the system's operational horizon from one month to four months.

This additional financial time dramatically changes the decision environment of the household.

If income is interrupted, the household does not immediately face urgent financial pressure. Instead, it has several months to evaluate the situation, assess the duration of the disturbance, and implement adjustments in a deliberate manner.

The emergency fund therefore converts stored liquidity into financial time.

This conversion preserves decision quality.

Without adequate runway, households must respond to disturbances immediately because obligations continue to arrive on schedule. Decisions must be made quickly in order to maintain operational continuity.

With extended runway, decisions can be evaluated sequentially rather than simultaneously.

The household can observe the nature of the disturbance, determine whether it is temporary or persistent, and choose responses that preserve the long-term stability of the financial structure.

This difference illustrates how emergency funds function as sources of financial time within the household financial system.

By extending financial runway, emergency funds preserve the time required for careful decision-making during periods of uncertainty.

The stability margin of a household financial system represents the distance between its current financial structure and the point at which obligations can no longer be sustained.

This margin is determined primarily by the amount of financial time available to absorb disturbances.

Emergency funds increase this margin.

When a household maintains dedicated emergency reserves, disturbances must exceed the capacity of that buffer before they begin to threaten the broader financial structure. The emergency fund absorbs the initial shock, allowing the system to continue operating without immediate structural change.

As a result, the financial system becomes more resilient.

Short-term disturbances remain contained within the buffer rather than propagating through the entire financial structure. Income fluctuations, unexpected expenses, or temporary disruptions can occur without forcing the household into immediate financial restructuring.

Without such reserves, the stability margin narrows significantly.

When unexpected events occur, the household must respond immediately because no dedicated liquidity layer exists to absorb the disturbance. Even small financial shocks can trigger rapid adjustments to obligations, spending patterns, or financial commitments.

In these conditions, decision compression becomes more likely.

Financial choices must be made quickly because the system lacks the time required for deliberate evaluation. The household may be forced to borrow funds, liquidate assets prematurely, or postpone essential payments in order to maintain operational continuity.

Each of these responses introduces additional structural pressures that may persist beyond the original disturbance.

Emergency funds reduce the likelihood of this outcome by expanding the stability margin of the system.

Because a buffer exists to absorb the initial shock, the household retains control over the pace and sequence of its financial responses. Decisions can be made deliberately rather than under immediate pressure.

This preservation of financial time for decision-making is the fundamental role of the emergency fund.

It does not eliminate uncertainty or prevent financial disturbances from occurring. Instead, it ensures that the system possesses sufficient financial time to manage those disturbances without losing operational control.

In this sense, the emergency fund functions as a stabilizing layer within the household financial structure.

By absorbing short-term shocks and extending financial runway, it preserves the conditions under which financial stability can be maintained.

Income Interruptions

Many household financial structures are built around the assumption that income will arrive continuously. Paychecks are expected to appear at regular intervals, and expenses are organized around that expectation. Housing payments, utilities, insurance premiums, and other obligations are scheduled according to predictable timelines that assume income will continue flowing into the system.

This expectation often works under normal conditions.

However, income continuity is not guaranteed. Across most careers, income flows experience periodic interruptions. Employment transitions occur, contract work includes gaps between projects, businesses experience fluctuations in revenue, and temporary disruptions to work can arise unexpectedly.

These interruptions do not necessarily represent financial failure. They are a common feature of income systems.

The stability of a household financial structure therefore depends not on whether income interruptions occur, but on whether the system is prepared to absorb them. Liquidity buffers and financial runway determine whether income interruptions remain temporary disturbances or evolve into destabilizing financial events.

Income volatility is often perceived as unusual or undesirable, but in practice it is a recurring feature of most income systems. Few careers maintain perfectly continuous income across long periods of time. Even stable employment environments experience transitions, interruptions, or fluctuations that temporarily alter income flows.

Job transitions are one of the most common examples.

When individuals move between positions, income may pause temporarily while the transition occurs. The period between the final payment from one employer and the first payment from another can create a gap in income even when the long-term career trajectory remains stable.

Contract and project-based work introduces similar patterns.

Many forms of professional work operate through discrete assignments rather than continuous employment. Projects may begin and end at different times, and the intervals between them can create temporary periods without income. These gaps are not necessarily signs of instability; they are structural characteristics of certain forms of employment.

Seasonal income fluctuations represent another source of volatility.

Some industries experience predictable cycles of activity throughout the year. Agricultural work, tourism, construction, and various service sectors may generate income during particular seasons while slowing during others. Households operating within these environments often experience natural income variations across the calendar year.

Temporary disruptions to employment can also interrupt income.

Health events, organizational changes, economic slowdowns, or operational disruptions may temporarily reduce working hours or pause income flows. In many cases these interruptions are short-lived, but they still alter the timing of financial resources entering the household system.

Income volatility is a recurring feature of many income systems.

The difficulty arises when households design their financial structures around the assumption of uninterrupted income. Expenses are scheduled based on predictable income flows, and little margin is built into the system to accommodate temporary gaps.

When an interruption occurs, the system must suddenly operate without the inflow of resources that normally sustain it.

The interruption itself may be temporary, but the absence of preparation can transform it into a destabilizing event.

The critical issue is therefore not the presence of income volatility but the financial system's capacity to tolerate it.

Households that maintain sufficient liquidity and financial runway treat income interruptions as manageable events within the broader financial structure. Households that lack such buffers experience the same interruptions as immediate financial pressure.

Understanding income volatility as a normal feature of financial life allows households to structure their liquidity systems accordingly.

When income stops temporarily, the household financial system encounters a structural imbalance.

Expenses continue to operate according to fixed timelines. Housing payments remain due, utilities must still be paid, and essential living costs continue regardless of whether income is currently flowing into the system.

Income, by contrast, becomes uncertain.

This mismatch between continuous expenses and interrupted income creates the central financial challenge associated with income interruptions. The household must continue meeting obligations while the primary source of financial inflow is temporarily absent.

In this environment, liquidity becomes the mechanism that sustains the system.

When income stops, the household begins to rely on existing financial resources in order to maintain operational continuity. These resources may include operating cash balances, emergency funds, or other accessible liquidity layers.

As these resources are used to meet expenses, the household begins consuming its financial runway.

The speed of this consumption depends on the household's burn rate.

Burn rate represents the pace at which expenses draw down available liquidity. Housing costs, food, transportation, insurance, and other recurring obligations determine how quickly the household's financial resources are used during periods without income.

If burn rate is relatively high, liquidity is consumed rapidly.

If burn rate is lower, the same amount of liquidity can sustain the system for a longer period.

This dynamic explains why income interruptions affect households differently even when the interruptions themselves are similar.

Two households may experience identical income gaps. One household may maintain sufficient liquidity to continue meeting obligations for several months, while the other may possess only a few weeks of operational capacity.

In the first case, the income interruption functions as a temporary financial adjustment.

In the second case, the interruption quickly produces financial pressure because the household's runway is consumed rapidly.

The key structural variable is therefore not the interruption itself but the system's ability to sustain operations during the interruption.

Liquidity buffers provide the resources that support this operational continuity. Without these buffers, the financial system immediately begins approaching the point at which obligations cannot be sustained.

As liquidity declines and obligations continue to arrive, the household faces increasing pressure to resolve the imbalance between income and expenses.

The longer the interruption persists, the more important the household's liquidity structure becomes.

If sufficient runway exists, the system continues operating while adjustments are considered. If runway is limited, the system approaches instability quickly as available resources decline.

Financial runway functions as the primary protective mechanism during income interruptions.

Runway measures the amount of financial time a household can continue operating when income becomes uncertain or temporarily stops. This financial time creates distance between the moment income is interrupted and the moment when obligations can no longer be sustained.

The presence of this buffer changes how income interruptions are experienced.

When runway is extended, the loss of income does not immediately destabilize the financial system. Instead, the household continues meeting its obligations using existing liquidity while evaluating the situation.

This financial time allows the household to respond deliberately.

Employment transitions can be managed without immediate financial pressure. Job searches can proceed methodically rather than urgently. Income arrangements can be negotiated, and opportunities can be evaluated carefully rather than accepted immediately due to financial constraints.

Runway therefore provides financial time for strategic decision-making.

Consider a simple illustration.

A household with $15,000 in accessible liquidity and a monthly burn rate of $3,000 possesses approximately five months of financial runway.

If income is interrupted, the household retains five months of operational time before the financial system reaches the point where obligations cannot be sustained.

During this period, the household can search for new employment, reorganize expenses, or explore alternative income sources without immediate financial pressure.

Now consider the same interruption occurring within a household possessing only $3,000 in liquidity with the same burn rate.

In this case, runway is approximately one month.

The household must resolve the income interruption quickly because obligations will exceed available resources within a short period. Decisions must occur rapidly, and the range of available options becomes narrower.

The interruption itself may be identical in both cases, but the financial experience differs dramatically.

Runway therefore determines whether income interruptions remain manageable or become destabilizing.

When sufficient runway exists, income gaps function as temporary disruptions that the financial system can absorb. When runway is limited, the same gaps immediately threaten the system's ability to sustain its obligations.

This distinction illustrates why liquidity buffers play such an important role in household financial stability.

By extending financial runway, liquidity systems provide the time required to manage income volatility without destabilizing the household's financial structure.

When income stops and liquidity is limited, the household financial system quickly approaches the conditions that produce decision compression.

Expenses continue to arrive according to fixed timelines, but the resources available to meet those expenses decline rapidly. As the financial runway shortens, the household must make decisions quickly in order to maintain operational continuity.

Under these conditions, the timing of financial decisions changes.

Instead of evaluating options carefully, households must respond immediately to approaching obligations. The primary objective becomes preserving short-term operational continuity rather than optimizing the long-term structure of the financial system.

This compressed decision environment often produces reactive choices.

Households may accept employment opportunities quickly even if those opportunities are not well aligned with their long-term plans.

They may borrow funds to meet immediate obligations, introducing commitments that persist beyond the income interruption.

They may also delay or restructure payments in ways that create additional financial pressure in the future.

Each of these decisions resolves an immediate problem but may introduce new constraints that affect the financial system later.

Liquidity buffers prevent this outcome by preserving financial time.

When income is interrupted but liquidity remains available, the household retains control over the timing of its decisions. Obligations can continue to be met while the household evaluates alternatives, gathers information, and determines the most appropriate response to the interruption.

This preservation of financial time protects decision quality.

Instead of responding to immediate pressure, households can assess the duration and severity of the income interruption before implementing structural changes. Adjustments can occur gradually rather than abruptly.

As a result, the interruption remains a temporary disturbance rather than a catalyst for cascading financial pressure.

Liquidity therefore transforms the experience of income loss.

Without liquidity, income interruptions quickly destabilize the financial system. Obligations exceed resources, financial runway disappears, and the household enters a compressed decision environment.

With liquidity, the same interruption becomes manageable.

Financial runway provides the time required to respond deliberately, preserving stability even while income remains uncertain.

In this way, liquidity systems help ensure that income interruptions remain temporary features of financial life rather than structural crises within the household financial system.

Expense Shock

Financial disturbances do not occur only through interruptions to income. Many disruptions originate on the expense side of the household financial system. Instead of income stopping or declining, the disturbance appears as a sudden increase in costs.

These events are commonly described as unexpected expenses.

Household financial systems regularly encounter such events. Repairs may be required, medical costs may appear suddenly, or obligations may arise that were not anticipated within the normal expense structure. These events introduce immediate financial pressure because they appear without advance scheduling.

Unlike routine expenses, which occur predictably within the household's financial cycle, these expenses arrive abruptly. The household must respond immediately because the obligation cannot always be delayed.

The financial impact of these disturbances depends on the structure of the household's liquidity system. When sufficient liquidity buffers exist, the system absorbs the expense without significant disruption. When liquidity is limited, the same event can rapidly reduce financial runway and place the household under financial pressure.

Understanding how expense shocks interact with liquidity layers is therefore essential for understanding the stability of household financial systems.

Household financial systems operate through predictable expense patterns. Many costs occur on regular schedules: housing payments, utilities, insurance premiums, and routine living expenses follow recurring timelines that allow households to organize their financial resources accordingly.

However, not all expenses follow predictable patterns.

Certain costs appear suddenly, often without advance warning. These sudden expense events introduce disturbances into the household financial structure because they require immediate resources that were not previously allocated within the system's normal expense cycle.

Vehicle repairs represent a common example.

Transportation systems occasionally require maintenance that cannot be postponed. Mechanical failures or accidents may require immediate repair in order to restore essential mobility. These costs may arise abruptly, and the household must allocate financial resources quickly in order to address them.

Medical costs present another example of sudden expenses.

Health-related events can introduce immediate financial obligations that were not anticipated within the household's regular budget. Even when insurance coverage exists, deductibles, co-payments, or uncovered services may require immediate payment.

Urgent home maintenance can produce similar financial disturbances.

Household infrastructure occasionally fails without warning. Plumbing issues, heating system failures, or structural repairs may require rapid attention to prevent further damage. These events often require resources before households have time to reorganize their finances.

Unexpected obligations may also emerge through administrative or contractual circumstances. Taxes, regulatory fees, or other financial commitments may appear suddenly if earlier estimates prove inaccurate or if conditions change.

These events share a common structural feature: they introduce expenses outside the household's normal financial schedule.

The disturbance itself is often temporary. A repair is completed, a medical cost is resolved, or an obligation is satisfied. However, the financial pressure occurs immediately because the expense arrives before the household has time to prepare.

This timing difference is what makes sudden expenses disruptive.

Routine expenses can be planned and distributed across time. Unexpected expenses appear suddenly and demand immediate financial resources.

The presence of such events does not indicate financial instability. Instead, they represent normal volatility within household financial systems.

The critical question is therefore not whether sudden expenses occur, but how the household system responds when they do.

Liquidity determines whether these events remain manageable disturbances or escalate into financial pressure that spreads through the system.

When an unexpected expense appears, the household financial system must respond immediately.

Unlike routine expenses, which are anticipated within the normal flow of income and spending, sudden expenses require resources that were not previously allocated. The household must therefore draw upon available liquidity to resolve the disturbance.

The first impact occurs within the system's most accessible liquidity.

Immediate cash balances typically absorb the earliest portion of the expense. Funds held within operational accounts are used to satisfy the obligation if they are sufficient to cover the cost.

If the expense exceeds the available operating cash, the system begins drawing upon additional liquidity buffers.

Emergency funds or other dedicated liquidity reserves provide the next layer of response. These buffers exist specifically to absorb financial disturbances that cannot be covered by routine operating cash.

As these buffers are used, the household's available liquidity declines.

This decline directly reduces the system's financial runway.

Runway measures how much financial time the household can continue operating without incoming income. When an unexpected expense consumes liquidity, the amount of operational time available within the financial system decreases.

Consider a simple illustration.

A household possesses $12,000 in accessible liquidity and a monthly burn rate of $3,000. Its financial runway is therefore approximately four months.

If an unexpected expense of $3,000 occurs, the household's remaining liquidity declines to $9,000.

With the same burn rate:

$9,000 liquidity

÷ $3,000 burn rate

Runway = 3 months

The expense shock has reduced the household's operational runway by one month.

This example illustrates how expense shocks propagate through the financial system.

The disturbance itself may be temporary, but its impact reduces the system's available financial time. If additional disturbances occur before liquidity is replenished, the household may approach the point where obligations cannot be sustained.

When liquidity buffers are limited, this process accelerates.

A sudden expense may consume a large portion of available liquidity, rapidly shortening the household's runway. As the stability margin narrows, the household may face increasing pressure to adjust its financial structure in order to maintain operational continuity.

Expense shocks therefore propagate by drawing down liquidity and reducing the time available for responding to future disturbances.

The speed of this propagation depends largely on the structure of the household's liquidity system.

The layered structure of liquidity plays an important role in managing expense shocks.

Because household financial systems contain multiple levels of liquidity, financial disturbances do not affect all resources simultaneously. Instead, the system absorbs pressure sequentially across different layers.

Immediate cash functions as the first line of response.

Funds held in operational accounts absorb the initial impact of the expense. Because these resources are already positioned within the household's day-to-day financial operations, they can be deployed instantly.

If the expense exceeds the available operating cash, the system begins to draw upon additional liquidity layers.

Emergency funds serve as the next layer of shock absorption. These funds are reserved specifically for disturbances that cannot be handled within the routine flow of financial transactions.

The presence of this emergency reserve allows the household to resolve sudden expenses without immediately disrupting other components of the financial structure.

If the disturbance exceeds the emergency buffer, deeper liquidity layers may become relevant.

Accessible capital, such as investments that can be converted into cash through transactions, may provide additional liquidity if the disturbance requires it. Because these resources typically require administrative steps to access, they function as slower but still available sources of financial support.

Convertible assets represent the deepest layer.

In extreme cases, households may consider restructuring long-term assets in order to generate liquidity. Because such actions involve significant structural change, they typically occur only when disturbances exceed the capacity of higher liquidity layers.

This layered structure distributes financial pressure across time.

Instead of forcing the household to access deep financial resources immediately, each layer absorbs a portion of the disturbance. The system gradually mobilizes resources as needed while maintaining operational continuity.

The benefit of this structure lies in its ability to slow the propagation of financial shocks.

A sudden expense does not immediately destabilize the entire financial system. Instead, the disturbance is absorbed progressively as the system moves through its liquidity layers.

This staged response preserves financial time.

By distributing pressure across multiple liquidity layers, the household retains the ability to evaluate its financial position and respond deliberately rather than reacting immediately to the disturbance.

Liquidity layers therefore function as structural shock absorbers within the household financial system.

The stability margin of a household financial system represents the distance between its current financial structure and the point where obligations can no longer be sustained.

Liquidity buffers determine the size of this margin.

When sufficient liquidity exists, sudden expenses remain contained within the system's financial buffers. The disturbance consumes a portion of available liquidity, but the household retains enough financial runway to maintain operational continuity.

In this situation, the expense shock functions as a temporary disturbance.

Once the obligation is resolved, the household may gradually rebuild its liquidity buffers while the financial system continues operating normally. The disturbance does not fundamentally alter the structure of the system.

However, when liquidity buffers are limited, the same expense shock can significantly reduce the household's stability margin.

Because the system possesses little financial runway, the sudden expense may consume a large portion of available resources. The household may approach the point where obligations cannot be sustained within a short period of time.

As this margin narrows, financial pressure increases.

The household may be forced to reorganize expenses quickly, access deeper liquidity layers, or introduce new obligations in order to maintain operational continuity.

These responses often occur within compressed decision environments where the timing of obligations leaves little room for careful evaluation.

The result is a shift from deliberate financial management to reactive financial response.

Liquidity buffers prevent this outcome by preserving the stability margin of the system.

When sufficient liquidity exists, unexpected expenses reduce financial runway but do not eliminate it. The household retains the time necessary to respond deliberately and restore balance within the financial structure.

In this way, liquidity determines how expense shocks are experienced.

Without liquidity, sudden expenses quickly destabilize the system. Financial runway disappears, and the household enters a compressed decision environment where urgent responses become necessary.

With liquidity, the same expenses remain manageable disturbances.

The system absorbs the shock, adjusts gradually, and maintains operational continuity.

Expense shocks therefore illustrate the central role liquidity plays within household financial stability.

They reveal how disturbances interact with the structure of financial resources — and how the presence or absence of liquidity determines whether those disturbances remain contained or propagate into broader financial instability.

How to Calculate Your Financial Runway

Household financial stability is often described through balances. Discussions frequently focus on how much money exists within the financial system—how much has been saved, how large an account balance may be, or how much value has accumulated across different assets.

While these measurements describe financial capacity, they do not fully capture the operational stability of the system.

Stability is better understood in terms of financial time.

When financial disturbances occur—whether through income interruptions or sudden expenses—the key question is not simply how much money remains. The more relevant question is how long the household can continue operating while the disturbance is resolved.

Financial runway converts liquidity into this measure of financial time.

Instead of describing financial strength purely through balances, runway expresses stability as financial time. It measures the time available between the moment income becomes uncertain and the point at which the household can no longer sustain its obligations.

Understanding how to estimate this duration allows households to evaluate the stability margin of their financial systems. It transforms liquidity from a static financial quantity into a time-based measure of operational survival.

Most financial measurements are expressed in monetary terms. Income is measured in dollars earned per month or year. Savings are measured in account balances. Assets are measured in total value.

These measurements describe the scale of a household's financial system, but they do not necessarily reveal how that system behaves during disruption.

When uncertainty appears—such as a temporary loss of income or a sudden increase in expenses—the household's immediate concern is not simply the size of its financial balances. Instead, the household must determine how long it can continue meeting obligations while the disturbance is addressed.

This is the financial time that financial runway measures.

Runway converts liquidity into a measure of financial time. Instead of asking how much money exists within the system, runway asks how long that money can sustain the system's operation.

This shift from balances to duration is important because financial disturbances unfold across time.

Income interruptions may last weeks or months before employment is restored. Unexpected expenses may temporarily disrupt the household's financial structure before stability returns. During these periods, the household must continue operating while the disturbance is resolved.

Financial runway measures the length of this financial horizon.

For example, two households may both hold $12,000 in liquid resources. From a purely financial perspective, their liquidity appears identical.

However, if one household requires $3,000 per month to sustain its essential expenses while the other requires $6,000 per month, their operational stability differs significantly.

In the first case, the liquidity provides four months of operational time.

In the second case, the same liquidity provides only two months of operational time.

The difference is not the amount of liquidity but the amount of time that liquidity can sustain the system.

Runway therefore reframes financial stability as a time-based concept.

It allows households to measure how long their financial systems can continue functioning under uncertainty. This measurement provides insight into how the system will behave during disturbances.

A longer runway indicates more financial time for responding to disruption.

A shorter runway indicates that the system may reach its operational limits quickly if income becomes uncertain.

By translating liquidity into time, financial runway makes the stability margin of the household financial system more visible.

Burn rate represents the pace at which a household's financial resources are consumed when income becomes uncertain or temporarily stops.

In practical terms, burn rate reflects the monthly level of expenses required to sustain the household's normal operations. Housing payments, food, transportation, insurance, and other essential costs determine how quickly liquidity reserves are used when income is absent.

Because these expenses occur regularly, burn rate functions as the operating speed of the financial system.

A system with a higher burn rate consumes liquidity quickly. A system with a lower burn rate consumes liquidity more slowly. This difference determines how efficiently liquidity is converted into financial time.

To illustrate this relationship, consider two households that possess identical liquidity reserves.

Each household holds $15,000 in accessible liquidity.

However, their burn rates differ.

Household A requires $3,000 per month to sustain essential expenses.

Household B requires $5,000 per month.

Applying the runway relationship:

$15,000 liquidity

÷ $3,000 burn rate

Runway = 5 months

For Household B:

$15,000 liquidity

÷ $5,000 burn rate

Runway = 3 months

Although both households possess the same amount of liquidity, the difference in burn rate produces a significant difference in operational financial time.

Household A can continue operating for five months without income.

Household B can continue operating for only three months under the same conditions.

This example illustrates how burn rate shapes the stability horizon of a household financial system.

Burn rate is largely determined by structural expenses. Housing costs, insurance obligations, transportation needs, and other essential expenses define the baseline level of financial activity required to maintain the household's operations.

Because many of these costs are fixed or semi-fixed, burn rate often remains relatively stable.

This stability makes burn rate a useful measurement for estimating how quickly liquidity will be consumed during financial disruptions.

When income interruptions occur or unexpected expenses appear, burn rate determines how rapidly the household's financial runway declines.

A higher burn rate reduces the amount of time available to respond to disturbances.

A lower burn rate allows liquidity reserves to sustain the system for longer periods.

In this way, burn rate functions as the denominator of financial runway.

It determines how quickly the household's stored liquidity is converted into operational financial time.

Once liquidity and burn rate are understood, estimating financial runway becomes a straightforward process.

The relationship can be expressed through a simple structural equation:

Runway = Liquidity ÷ Burn Rate

In this relationship, liquidity represents the financial resources that can be accessed quickly when income becomes uncertain. These resources typically include cash balances, emergency funds, and other liquid financial reserves that can be used without complex transactions.

Burn rate represents the monthly level of expenses required to sustain the household's operations.

Dividing liquidity by burn rate converts financial resources into a measure of financial time.

For example, consider a household with $12,000 in accessible liquidity and monthly essential expenses of $3,000.

$12,000 liquidity

÷ $3,000 burn rate

Runway = 4 months

This calculation indicates that the household can continue operating for approximately four months without incoming income.

If liquidity increases while burn rate remains constant, the runway extends.

For instance:

$18,000 liquidity

÷ $3,000 burn rate

Runway = 6 months

In this case, the additional liquidity expands the household's operational horizon by two months.

Alternatively, if burn rate increases while liquidity remains unchanged, the runway shortens.

For example:

$12,000 liquidity

÷ $4,000 burn rate

Runway = 3 months

The higher burn rate reduces the amount of time the system can sustain operations under income uncertainty.

These simple calculations show how liquidity and expenses interact to determine the financial time available within the household system.

Rather, they provide a conceptual framework for understanding how long the household can continue operating if income becomes uncertain.

By expressing financial capacity in terms of time rather than balances, runway calculations allow households to visualize their financial time horizon.

This horizon helps determine how the system will behave during financial disturbances.

Financial runway ultimately represents the financial survival distance of the household financial system.

This distance measures how far the system can travel through a period of uncertainty before its liquidity resources are exhausted. It reflects the amount of financial time available for responding to disturbances such as income interruptions or unexpected expenses.

When runway is long, the household possesses substantial survival distance.

Financial disturbances can occur without immediately threatening the system's ability to sustain its obligations. The household retains time to evaluate options, reorganize expenses gradually, and restore income flows without immediate financial pressure.

This extended time horizon protects the stability margin of the system.

The stability margin represents the distance between the current financial structure and the point where obligations can no longer be sustained. A longer runway increases this margin by expanding the amount of time available for adjustment.

When runway is short, the survival distance of the system is limited.

Even relatively small disturbances can quickly consume the available liquidity. As the runway shortens, the household approaches the point where financial obligations cannot be met without structural change.

This environment increases the likelihood of decision compression.

Because financial time is limited, the household must respond quickly to disturbances. Decisions that would normally be evaluated carefully must instead be made under time pressure in order to maintain operational continuity.

Runway calculations reveal where the system stands relative to this threshold.

By measuring liquidity in terms of operational time, households gain visibility into how long their financial structures can sustain uncertainty. This visibility allows the stability margin of the system to be understood more clearly.

Financial stability, in this sense, becomes a question of financial time rather than simply a question of money.

The more financial time the system possesses, the greater its capacity to absorb disturbances without becoming destabilizing.

Runway provides the measurement of that time.

Stability Margins

Financial stability is often described in immediate terms. A household is considered stable if it can meet its current obligations. Bills are paid on time, income covers expenses, and the financial system appears to function normally.

However, this perspective captures only the present moment.

A household may be meeting its obligations today while still operating close to the point where those obligations could no longer be sustained. Another household may be meeting the same obligations while possessing substantial distance from that threshold.

Both households appear stable in the present, but their underlying financial structures differ significantly.

The difference lies in the distance between the current financial position and the point where the system would fail.

This distance is the stability margin.

The stability margin represents how far a household financial system can move through uncertainty before obligations can no longer be sustained. It reflects the amount of financial time available to absorb disturbances before the system reaches its operational limits.

Financial runway determines the size of this margin.

A longer runway increases the distance between the present moment and financial instability. A shorter runway reduces that distance and brings the household closer to the point where financial pressure becomes unavoidable.

Understanding stability in terms of margins rather than immediate balances provides a clearer view of how household financial systems behave under uncertainty.

Financial stability is rarely a binary condition.

Households do not typically move directly from a stable financial position to immediate failure. Instead, financial systems tend to progress gradually toward instability as liquidity declines and operational flexibility diminishes.

An unexpected expense may reduce available liquidity. A temporary income disruption may consume a portion of the household's financial reserves. These events do not necessarily destabilize the system immediately, but they move the household closer to the point where obligations could become difficult to sustain.

As liquidity declines, the system's financial runway shortens.

Each reduction in runway decreases the amount of time available to respond to future disturbances. The household may still appear stable because obligations continue to be met, but the distance between the present financial position and the system's operational limit becomes smaller.

The stability margin measures this distance.

It reflects how much financial time remains before the system reaches the point where obligations cannot be sustained without structural change.

When the stability margin is large, disturbances must accumulate over a long period before the system approaches instability. The household possesses sufficient financial time to absorb disruptions and restore balance within the financial structure.

When the margin is small, the system operates close to its operational limits. Even modest disturbances may bring the household near the point where obligations can no longer be maintained.

This gradual movement toward instability helps explain why financial pressure often appears to build over time.

A household may experience several small disturbances that individually appear manageable. However, each disturbance reduces liquidity and shortens financial runway. Over time, the accumulation of these events narrows the stability margin.

Eventually the system may reach a point where even minor disruptions produce immediate financial pressure.

Understanding stability as a distance rather than a condition helps clarify this process.

Households do not simply move from stable to unstable. They move along a continuum defined by the size of their stability margin.

Runway determines how wide that margin is.

Financial runway determines how much distance exists between the household's current financial position and the threshold of instability.

When runway is long, the stability margin expands.

A household with substantial runway possesses significant financial time before obligations become unsustainable. This time creates distance between disturbances and structural instability.

When disturbances shocks occur, the system absorbs them gradually.

An unexpected expense may reduce liquidity, but the household still retains sufficient runway to maintain operations. An income interruption may consume several weeks of financial time, yet the system remains far from the point where obligations cannot be met.

Because the margin remains wide, the financial structure retains flexibility.

The household can respond to disturbances deliberately. Adjustments to expenses can be implemented gradually. Employment transitions can be managed without immediate pressure. Financial decisions occur within a time horizon that allows careful evaluation.

This deliberate pace preserves system stability.

Disturbances remain contained because they occur within a structure that possesses ample financial time. Instead of producing urgent financial pressure, disruptions are absorbed and distributed across the available runway.

In effect, runway acts as a structural distance within the financial system.

The greater the amount of runway, the farther the household stands from the threshold where obligations can no longer be sustained.

This distance changes how financial disturbances are experienced.

For households with wide stability margins, disruptions rarely threaten the overall structure of the system. The financial system continues operating while adjustments are implemented.

For households with limited margins, the same disturbances may quickly produce financial pressure because the system has little time to respond.

Runway therefore transforms the financial environment in which decisions occur.

When financial time is abundant, the household operates within a stable decision environment. When financial time is scarce, the environment becomes increasingly sensitive to disturbances.

Expanding runway increases the margin that protects the system from instability.

When financial runway becomes short, the stability margin narrows.

In these systems, the distance between the household's current financial position and the threshold of instability becomes small. Liquidity buffers are limited, and the system possesses little financial time to absorb disturbances.

This narrow margin increases financial fragility.

Even small disruptions can move the system close to its operational limits. An unexpected expense may consume a large portion of available liquidity. A temporary income interruption may rapidly reduce the household's ability to sustain its obligations.

Because the margin is already narrow, these disturbances push the system toward instability quickly.

Households operating within narrow margins often appear stable during normal conditions. Income may cover expenses, and obligations may be met on schedule. However, the absence of substantial liquidity reserves means that the system lacks protection against uncertainty.

The stability visible in the present moment depends on the continuation of favorable conditions.

When those conditions change, the system has little room to adjust.

This environment increases the likelihood of decision compression.

As financial runway declines, the time available to evaluate financial choices disappears. Obligations continue to arrive on fixed schedules, but the resources required to meet those obligations are diminishing.

The household must respond quickly in order to maintain operational continuity.

Financial decisions that would normally be evaluated over weeks or months must be made within days. Options that require time to develop may no longer be feasible because the system lacks the operational horizon required to support them.

The result is a shift toward reactive financial behavior.

Instead of choosing the most stable long-term solution, households may choose the fastest available solution in order to resolve immediate pressure. Borrowing, delayed payments, or rapid asset sales may provide short-term relief but introduce new constraints into the financial system.

These responses often further narrow the stability margin.

New obligations increase burn rate. Reduced liquidity shortens runway. Each reactive decision moves the system closer to the threshold of instability.

Narrow margins therefore create a feedback loop of financial fragility.

Without sufficient runway, disturbances propagate quickly through the financial structure and accelerate the movement toward instability.

Households frequently assess their financial position by looking at the amount of savings they possess or the value of their assets. While these measurements provide useful information, they do not fully describe the resilience of the financial system.

Stability is better understood as distance rather than balance.

The relevant question is not simply how much money exists within the system but how far the system stands from the point where obligations could no longer be sustained.

Two households may possess identical savings balances while occupying very different positions along this distance.

Consider two households that each hold $12,000 in accessible liquidity.

The first household has essential expenses of $3,000 per month. The second household has expenses of $6,000 per month.

Although their liquidity balances are identical, their financial runway differs.

For the first household:

$12,000 liquidity

÷ $3,000 burn rate

Runway = 4 months

For the second household:

$12,000 liquidity

÷ $6,000 burn rate

Runway = 2 months

The first household possesses twice the operational financial time of the second household.

As a result, the stability margin of the first system is significantly larger.

If disturbances occur, the first household has more time to respond before obligations become unsustainable. The second household operates closer to the threshold of instability because its runway is shorter.

This example illustrates why stability cannot be evaluated solely through balances.

Liquidity, burn rate, and financial structure together determine how much financial time exists within the system. That time defines the distance between the present moment and potential instability.

Runway therefore functions as a measure of financial resilience.

By converting liquidity into time, runway reveals how much distance the system possesses before reaching its operational limits. The larger this distance, the greater the household's capacity to absorb disturbances without destabilizing.

In this sense, financial stability emerges not from the size of financial balances alone but from the amount of financial time those balances can create.

The stability margin expresses that financial time as distance.

Stability margins therefore determine how much uncertainty a household can tolerate before financial pressure begins to appear.

Understanding how these margins expand or contract requires examining the ways households structure their liquidity over time.

Liquidity Tradeoffs

Liquidity plays a central role in household financial stability. It provides the financial time required to absorb disturbances, maintain operational continuity, and avoid the compressed decision environments that often destabilize financial systems.

However, maintaining liquidity also involves an inherent tradeoff.

Resources held in liquid form are typically not deployed into long-term assets that may produce higher investment growth. Funds retained as cash or savings remain available for immediate use, but they may not generate the same level of return as capital invested in long-duration assets.

Households therefore face a structural choice within their financial systems.

Liquidity improves stability by extending financial runway and expanding the stability margin. Yet holding liquidity also reduces the amount of capital available for long-term growth.

This tension between stability and growth is one of the central tradeoffs within household financial structures. Understanding how this tradeoff operates—and how households balance it—is essential for maintaining both operational resilience and long-term financial development.

Liquidity provides immediate accessibility. Funds held in liquid form can be deployed quickly to meet financial obligations, absorb disturbances, or sustain operations during periods of uncertainty. This accessibility is what allows liquidity to create financial time.

However, accessibility often comes at the cost of lower financial returns.

Liquid assets typically prioritize safety and availability over growth. Funds held in checking accounts, savings accounts, or similar instruments remain available for immediate use but usually produce modest financial returns relative to assets designed for long-term accumulation.

The difference between these uses of capital creates an opportunity cost.

When funds are held as liquidity reserves, they are not simultaneously invested in assets that may produce higher returns over time. The household effectively exchanges potential financial growth for increased operational stability.

This exchange represents a deliberate structural choice.

By maintaining liquidity, the household ensures that financial disturbances can be absorbed without destabilizing the system. The presence of accessible resources protects the household from entering compressed decision environments when unexpected events occur.

At the same time, these reserves remain idle from the standpoint of long-term financial accumulation.

The opportunity cost of liquidity reflects the difference between two possible uses of capital: immediate accessibility or long-term growth.

Neither function is inherently superior. Each serves a different role within the financial system.

Liquidity protects the operational stability of the household during periods of uncertainty. Long-term assets increase financial capacity over extended time horizons.

Because both functions are important, the financial system must balance them.

Excessive emphasis on liquidity may reduce the household's ability to accumulate wealth over time. Excessive emphasis on investment may increase financial growth while simultaneously reducing the system's capacity to withstand disturbances.

The challenge lies in maintaining enough liquidity to protect stability while still allowing resources to participate in long-term financial development.

This balance is the essence of the liquidity tradeoff.

The tension between investment and liquidity becomes visible when households allocate their financial resources.

Long-term investments often promise higher potential returns than liquid assets. Capital placed into businesses, real estate, equities, or other long-duration assets may appreciate over time and increase the household's total financial capacity.

From the perspective of wealth accumulation, allocating resources toward these assets can appear attractive.

However, these assets often require time to convert into usable funds.

Real estate may require sale transactions. Investment portfolios may need to be liquidated through financial markets. Business assets may require negotiations with buyers or restructuring of ownership.

During stable periods, these limitations may appear insignificant. The household's financial system operates normally because income covers expenses and obligations are satisfied on schedule.

The limitations of liquidity become visible only when disturbances occur.

If income becomes uncertain or unexpected expenses arise, the household must access financial resources quickly. When a large portion of the household's wealth exists in long-term investments, those resources may not be immediately available.

This situation illustrates the liquidity–investment tradeoff.

Allocating capital entirely toward long-term assets may increase total wealth while simultaneously reducing operational flexibility. The household's balance sheet may appear strong, but its liquidity reserves may be insufficient to absorb financial disturbances.

The result is a financial structure that appears wealthy but operates with limited financial time.

In such systems, even temporary disruptions can create immediate financial pressure. Because liquidity buffers are small, the household must quickly convert investments into usable funds or introduce new financial obligations to maintain operations.

These responses often occur under decision compression.

The tradeoff reflects two different dimensions of financial strength.

Investment capacity increases the long-term growth potential of the financial system. Liquidity preserves the system's ability to withstand short-term uncertainty.

Both forms of financial strength are valuable, but they serve different roles.

A system designed solely for growth may lack the flexibility required to remain stable during disturbances. A system designed solely for liquidity may remain stable but grow more slowly over time.

The challenge is not choosing one objective over the other, but understanding how both interact within the household financial structure.

Liquidity tradeoffs become particularly visible when wealth accumulates in assets that cannot easily be converted into usable financial resources.

These situations can be described as household liquidity traps.

A liquidity trap occurs when a household possesses significant financial value but lacks the accessible resources required to generate financial time during disturbances. The wealth exists within the system, yet the system cannot mobilize that wealth quickly enough to maintain operational continuity.

This condition often emerges when assets become concentrated in illiquid forms.

Residential property provides a common example.

Home equity may represent a large portion of household wealth, yet converting that equity into usable liquidity often requires refinancing, borrowing, or selling the property. Each of these processes requires time and may depend on external financial conditions.

Similarly, retirement accounts may hold substantial financial value but remain restricted by tax rules or administrative constraints that limit immediate access.

Business ownership can produce similar dynamics.

A household may possess valuable ownership stakes in a business, yet those assets may not be easily converted into cash without complex transactions or negotiations.

In each case, the household appears financially strong from the perspective of net worth. However, the operational liquidity available within the system may remain limited.

This imbalance introduces structural fragility.

When disturbances occur, the household cannot immediately deploy its financial resources because those resources are embedded in assets that require time to access. The system therefore behaves as though much of its wealth were temporarily unavailable.

The presence of illiquid wealth does not eliminate financial pressure during disturbances. Instead, it may intensify that pressure because the household must navigate complex processes to access the resources needed to maintain stability.

Liquidity traps illustrate the difference between financial value and financial time.

Value reflects the total resources contained within the system. Financial time reflects how quickly those resources can be used to sustain operations.

When assets become trapped in illiquid forms, the system may contain substantial value while still lacking the time required to absorb disturbances.

Because of the tradeoffs between liquidity and investment, stable household financial systems typically maintain a dedicated liquidity layer within the broader financial structure.

This layer exists specifically to preserve operational flexibility.

While long-term investments contribute to wealth accumulation, liquidity reserves provide the financial time required to navigate uncertainty. By maintaining accessible resources, the household ensures that disturbances can be absorbed without immediately restructuring its long-term financial assets.

This separation between liquidity and investment serves an important stabilizing function.

When financial disturbances occur, the household can rely on its liquidity layer to sustain operations while evaluating appropriate responses. Long-term investments remain intact, and decisions about those assets can be made deliberately rather than under immediate financial pressure.

The liquidity layer therefore protects the household from being forced into premature asset liquidation.

Without such a buffer, the household may need to sell investments quickly in order to generate liquidity. Rapid sales often occur under unfavorable conditions and may compromise long-term financial objectives.

Maintaining a liquidity layer prevents this outcome by ensuring that immediate financial needs can be addressed without disturbing the broader financial structure.

This approach reflects a systems perspective on financial stability.

Liquidity should not be viewed as idle capital that simply fails to produce growth. Instead, it functions as an operational component of the financial system—one that preserves the system's ability to absorb disturbances and maintain control over financial decisions.

The presence of liquidity increases financial time.

Financial time protects the stability margin of the household system, allowing disturbances to be managed without destabilizing the structure that supports long-term financial growth.

In this sense, liquidity and investment perform complementary roles.

Investment expands the financial capacity of the system over time. Liquidity protects the system's ability to navigate uncertainty along the way.

Stable financial systems therefore maintain both liquidity and investment capacity.

Liquidity provides the time required to sustain stability. Investments provide the growth that shapes the system's long-term trajectory.

Understanding how households maintain this balance over time requires examining how financial runway expands and contracts as liquidity is rebuilt after disturbances.

How Runway Shapes Financial Decisions

Financial systems are not abstract mechanisms operating in isolation. They are structures within which households make decisions. Every financial choice—whether related to spending, employment, borrowing, or restructuring obligations—occurs within the constraints created by the household's financial architecture.

Because of this relationship, the structure of a financial system influences the behavior of the people operating within it.

Liquidity and financial runway determine how much financial time the system contains. That time does not only influence mechanical outcomes such as the ability to pay obligations. It also shapes the decision environment in which financial choices occur.

When financial time is abundant, decisions can be evaluated carefully. When financial time becomes scarce, the environment shifts toward urgency.

The decision environment therefore changes as runway expands or contracts.

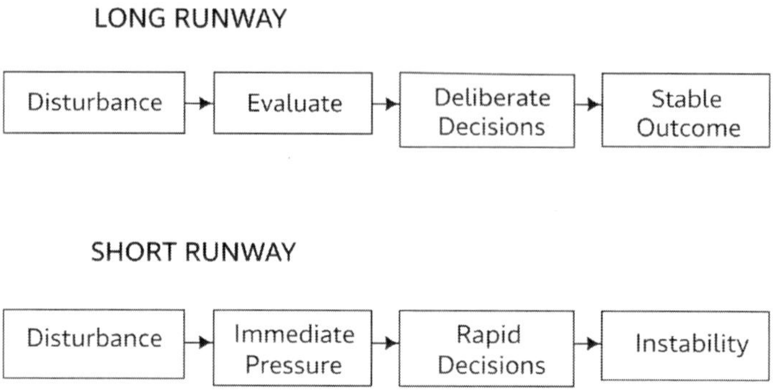

[Diagram 4 — Financial Runway and Decision Environment]

Financial time creates decision space.

When households possess substantial financial runway, the interval between financial disturbances and the point where obligations become unsustainable is relatively long. This interval provides the time necessary to observe conditions, gather information, and evaluate potential responses.

Within this environment, financial decisions occur more deliberately.

Households can consider multiple alternatives before selecting a course of action. The timing of decisions can be aligned with the availability of information rather than with the arrival of immediate financial pressure. Choices can be evaluated in terms of long-term consequences rather than solely in terms of short-term survival.

This decision space changes the nature of financial behavior.

When time is available, households can compare options across multiple dimensions. They may evaluate employment opportunities based on long-term compatibility rather than immediate necessity. They may restructure expenses gradually instead of implementing abrupt financial adjustments.

Because decisions are not forced by urgency, the household retains control over the pace of its financial responses.

Financial runway therefore expands the decision horizon of the household system.

The longer the runway, the greater the capacity to analyze situations before acting. This expanded horizon allows households to integrate broader considerations into their decisions, including long-term financial goals, contractual obligations, and structural stability.

In effect, financial time creates the conditions necessary for deliberate decision-making.

The presence of this time does not guarantee that every decision will be optimal. However, it ensures that decisions occur within an environment where evaluation is possible.

When financial systems operate within wide stability margins, disturbances do not immediately threaten operational continuity. The household can respond to uncertainty with analysis rather than urgency.

This relationship illustrates an important behavioral consequence of financial runway.

Financial time does not simply allow households to pay obligations. It allows them to think before they act.

When financial runway becomes short, the decision environment changes.

As liquidity declines and the stability margin narrows, the household begins to operate within a compressed time horizon. Obligations continue to arrive on fixed schedules while the resources available to meet those obligations diminish.

This narrowing of financial time alters the decision environment.

Under these conditions, urgency becomes the dominant feature of the decision environment. The household no longer possesses the time necessary to evaluate alternatives carefully. Instead, financial choices must be made quickly in order to maintain operational continuity.

This shift produces what can be described as decision compression.

In compressed environments, the number of viable options often appears smaller. Decisions that would normally require time to develop—such as negotiating new income arrangements or reorganizing long-term obligations—may no longer appear feasible because the system lacks the operational horizon required to support them.

As a result, the decision process becomes simplified.

Instead of evaluating multiple alternatives, households often focus on resolving the most immediate financial pressure. The objective becomes preventing the next disruption rather than optimizing the long-term structure of the financial system.

The psychological effect of this compression can be significant.

When time is limited, attention narrows toward the most urgent financial obligations. Future considerations become secondary because the immediate problem requires resolution.

This narrowing of focus is not irrational. It reflects the structural constraints imposed by the financial system.

When obligations must be met within a short timeframe, the household must prioritize speed over evaluation. Decisions that might otherwise be postponed until additional information becomes available must instead be made immediately.

The result is a decision environment dominated by urgency rather than analysis.

This environment can influence how households perceive risk, opportunity, and acceptable outcomes. Options that would normally be rejected may appear acceptable if they provide immediate relief from financial pressure.

Decision compression therefore alters both the timing and the character of financial choices.

As financial time disappears, the household's capacity for deliberate evaluation diminishes.

When households operate with limited financial runway, the compressed decision environment often produces reactive financial behavior.

Reactive decisions are not necessarily poor decisions in the moment. In many cases they represent rational responses to immediate financial pressure. However, because these decisions prioritize short-term resolution, they may introduce longer-term consequences that affect the stability of the financial system.

One common response to compressed decision environments is the acceptance of unfavorable financial arrangements.

When time is limited, households may agree to terms that they would otherwise evaluate more carefully. Employment opportunities may be accepted quickly even if they are not well aligned with long-term career plans. Contractual arrangements may be accepted because they provide immediate income rather than because they represent the most advantageous option.

Borrowing under pressure represents another frequent behavioral response.

When liquidity is insufficient to meet immediate obligations, households may seek external financing to maintain operational continuity. Borrowing provides rapid access to financial resources, but it also introduces future repayment obligations that may increase financial pressure later.

In compressed environments, the speed of access often outweighs the long-term cost of the borrowing arrangement.

Asset liquidation can produce similar patterns.

When financial time disappears, households may sell investments or other assets quickly in order to generate liquidity. Rapid asset sales may occur under unfavorable conditions because the household cannot wait for better opportunities to convert those assets into cash.

Each of these behaviors resolves an immediate problem.

However, the cumulative effect of such decisions can gradually alter the structure of the household financial system. New obligations may increase financial commitments, reduced assets may diminish long-term capacity, and unfavorable arrangements may constrain future choices.

These consequences are not necessarily the result of poor judgment.

They are often the predictable outcome of operating within a financial system that lacks sufficient time for deliberate decision-making.

Limited runway therefore shapes financial behavior by constraining the environment in which decisions occur.

When the stability margin is narrow, households must respond quickly to preserve operational continuity. This urgency often produces decisions that resolve the present disturbance but reduce flexibility in the future.

Financial runway is typically described in mechanical terms. It measures the amount of time a household can continue operating when income becomes uncertain or when financial disturbances occur.

However, runway also plays a psychological role within the financial system.

By preserving financial time, liquidity buffers protect the quality of financial decision-making.

When households maintain sufficient runway, disturbances do not immediately threaten operational continuity. Obligations can continue to be met while the household evaluates potential responses.

This environment reduces the urgency associated with financial decisions.

Instead of responding to immediate pressure, households can approach financial problems with a longer time horizon. Options can be compared, information can be gathered, and potential consequences can be evaluated before action is taken.

The result is a more stable decision environment.

Within this environment, households retain control over the timing of their financial responses. Decisions occur deliberately rather than reactively, and adjustments to the financial structure can be implemented gradually.

Over time, this preservation of decision quality contributes to the overall stability of the household financial system.

Because decisions are made with sufficient time for evaluation, they are more likely to support the long-term structure of the system rather than merely resolving immediate financial pressure.

Liquidity therefore serves a dual function.

Mechanically, it provides the resources necessary to sustain operations during financial disturbances. Psychologically, it preserves the decision environment required for deliberate financial management.

These two functions are closely connected.

Financial time allows households not only to maintain operational continuity but also to maintain clarity in their decision-making processes.

When financial runway is preserved, households remain in control of their financial decisions even during periods of uncertainty.

In this sense, liquidity does more than stabilize financial system.

It stabilizes the environment in which financial decisions are made.

Runway Erosion

Financial instability rarely appears without warning. In most cases, the financial structure of a household does not move directly from stability to crisis through a single event. Instead, the transition toward instability often occurs gradually as the conditions supporting financial stability change over time.

One of the most common ways this occurs is through the slow erosion of financial runway.

Household financial systems are dynamic. Income may grow, consumption patterns may change, and long-term obligations may gradually expand as households adapt their lifestyles. These changes do not necessarily appear risky in the moment. Each adjustment may seem manageable when evaluated individually.

However, the cumulative effect of these adjustments can alter the underlying structure of the financial system.

As expenses increase, the burn rate of the household rises. If liquidity reserves do not expand at the same pace, the system begins to lose financial runway. The stability margin gradually narrows.

This process is often difficult to detect because it develops slowly.

Unlike sudden disturbances such as income interruptions or expense shocks, runway erosion rarely produces immediate pressure. The household continues meeting its obligations, and the financial system appears to function normally.

Yet beneath the surface, the stability margin is shrinking.

Understanding how runway erodes, and how households can maintain awareness of this process, is essential for preserving long-term financial stability.

Financial runway represents the amount of time a household can sustain its financial obligations during periods of uncertainty. When runway is long, the household retains substantial operational flexibility. When runway shortens, the system moves closer to the point where disturbances may produce financial pressure.

One of the most important characteristics of runway erosion is its gradual nature.

Unlike sudden financial shocks, runway erosion often develops without a clear triggering event. Instead, the household's financial structure changes incrementally over time.

Expenses may increase slightly each year. New commitments may be added gradually. Lifestyle adjustments may introduce additional financial obligations that become part of the system's regular burn rate.

Each individual change may appear small relative to the overall financial structure.

However, these changes affect the pace at which liquidity is consumed when income becomes uncertain. As burn rate increases, the amount of financial time provided by existing liquidity reserves declines.

This relationship can be illustrated with a simple example.

Consider a household with $18,000 in accessible liquidity and monthly essential expenses of $3,000.

$18,000 liquidity

÷ $3,000 burn rate

Runway = 6 months

Over time, the household's expenses gradually increase. Housing costs rise, additional services are adopted, and recurring expenses expand.

The new burn rate becomes $4,500 per month.

$18,000 liquidity

÷ $4,500 burn rate

Runway = 4 months

Although the household's liquidity reserves remain unchanged, financial runway has declined from six months to four months.

This gradual change illustrates the core mechanism of runway erosion.

The financial system continues functioning normally, but the distance between the present financial structure and potential instability becomes smaller.

Because the erosion occurs slowly, it often goes unnoticed.

Households typically observe their financial position through balances rather than through operational duration. If savings remain constant or increase modestly, the system may appear stable even as the underlying burn rate accelerates.

Runway erosion therefore occurs quietly.

The system remains operational, but its capacity to absorb future disturbances declines.

Over time, this gradual loss of financial time can significantly alter the stability margin of the household financial system.

Runway erosion is closely connected to the way household lifestyles evolve over time.

As income grows or financial conditions improve, households often expand their consumption patterns. These adjustments may enhance comfort, convenience, or perceived quality of life. In many cases they appear financially manageable because they occur gradually and often accompany rising income.

However, each adjustment modifies the structure of the household financial system.

One common example involves housing commitments.

A household may choose to move into a larger home or assume a more expensive housing arrangement. While the decision may align with current income levels, the resulting increase in housing costs becomes a permanent component of the household's burn rate.

Over time, this structural obligation reduces the flexibility of the financial system.

Recurring service expenses can produce similar effects.

Subscriptions, service contracts, maintenance agreements, and other recurring costs may accumulate gradually. Each additional obligation increases the monthly expenses that must be sustained regardless of future financial conditions.

Discretionary spending patterns can also expand over time.

Dining, travel, entertainment, and other lifestyle expenditures may increase as households adapt their consumption patterns to higher income levels. While these expenses may appear optional, they often become embedded within the household's routine financial structure.

Long-term contractual obligations further reinforce these changes.

Financing arrangements, leases, and service agreements create fixed commitments that persist over extended periods. Once established, these obligations contribute to the household's burn rate regardless of future financial circumstances.

The cumulative effect of these adjustments is an increase in the household's structural expenses.

As burn rate increases, the financial system requires greater liquidity reserves to maintain the same level of operational runway. If liquidity does not expand accordingly, the system gradually loses financial time.

This process often occurs without immediate awareness.

Each individual adjustment appears manageable because it reflects current financial conditions. However, the accumulation of these adjustments changes the relationship between expenses and liquidity.

Over time, the household may discover that the financial time once provided by its liquidity reserves has diminished significantly.

Lifestyle expansion therefore represents one of the most common drivers of runway erosion.

As burn rate increases and runway declines, the stability margin of the household financial system narrows.

The stability margin represents the operational distance between the household's current financial structure and the point where obligations can no longer be sustained. This distance is measured in financial time.

When runway is long, the stability margin is wide. The household can absorb disturbances while maintaining operational continuity.

When runway shortens, the margin becomes narrower.

Even if the household's liquidity reserves remain unchanged, the increase in burn rate reduces the amount of time those reserves can sustain the system during uncertainty.

This compression changes how the financial system responds to disturbances.

When margins are wide, financial shocks remain relatively distant from the threshold of instability. Unexpected expenses or temporary income disruptions may reduce liquidity but do not immediately threaten the system's ability to sustain its obligations.

The household retains sufficient time to evaluate responses and restore balance.

When margins become narrow, the same disturbances produce more immediate pressure.

Because the household possesses less financial time, even modest shocks can move the system close to the point where obligations become difficult to sustain. The system becomes more sensitive to volatility.

As financial time declines, households may find themselves responding more quickly to disturbances that previously would have been absorbed comfortably. Financial decisions must be made sooner because the system possesses less operational distance before reaching its limits.

The result is a financial structure that appears stable under normal conditions but reacts strongly to disruption.

This pattern illustrates how stability margin compression gradually alters the resilience of the household financial system.

The system may appear unchanged on the surface, yet its ability to absorb disturbances has weakened.

Small shocks that once remained manageable may now produce significant financial pressure.

Runway erosion does not simply reduce financial flexibility.

It changes the system's sensitivity to uncertainty.

Because runway erosion often develops gradually, maintaining financial stability requires active oversight of the relationship between burn rate and liquidity reserves.

This oversight is referred to as liquidity governance.

Liquidity governance refers to the ongoing management of the financial system's operational time. It involves maintaining awareness of how structural expenses interact with available liquidity and how changes in lifestyle or financial commitments affect the household's runway.

Without this awareness, runway erosion can occur quietly.

As expenses expand, the household's burn rate increases. If liquidity reserves remain unchanged, the amount of financial time available during uncertainty declines.

Because the system continues operating normally, this erosion may remain unnoticed until a financial disturbance occurs.

When disturbances eventually appear, the household may discover that the stability margin has narrowed significantly.

Maintaining liquidity governance helps prevent this outcome.

By monitoring the relationship between expenses and reserves, households can observe how structural changes affect financial runway. Lifestyle adjustments can be evaluated not only in terms of their immediate affordability but also in terms of their effect on the system's operational horizon.

This perspective encourages a broader view of financial stability.

The question is not simply whether a new expense can be supported by current income. It is whether the addition of that expense alters the balance between burn rate and liquidity in a way that reduces the system's financial time.

When liquidity governance is active, households remain aware of these dynamics.

Runway becomes a structural metric that informs financial decisions. Changes in lifestyle, contractual obligations, or financial commitments can be evaluated in terms of how they affect the stability margin of the system.

In this way, liquidity governance preserves financial time.

By maintaining alignment between burn rate and liquidity reserves, the household protects the runway that allows uncertainty to be absorbed without destabilizing the financial structure.

The goal is to ensure that those changes do not quietly erode the financial time that protects stability.

When runway erosion continues long enough, the household eventually approaches a point where financial disturbances can no longer be absorbed comfortably. Understanding how systems recover from that position requires examining how financial runway can be rebuilt once it has been depleted.

Liquidity Traps

Financial value and financial liquidity are often treated as interchangeable concepts. When households accumulate assets or increase their net worth, it is commonly assumed that financial stability has improved accordingly. The presence of valuable assets appears to indicate financial strength.

However, value and liquidity are not identical.

Assets represent stored financial value, but that value may not be immediately accessible when the system requires it. Some assets can be converted into usable funds quickly, while others require time, transactions, or external conditions before they can provide financial support.

This distinction creates the possibility of liquidity traps.

A household may appear financially secure when measured through net worth or asset ownership while simultaneously lacking the accessible liquidity required to sustain operations during financial disturbances. When disruption occurs, the system may contain significant value but still lack the financial time necessary to respond effectively.

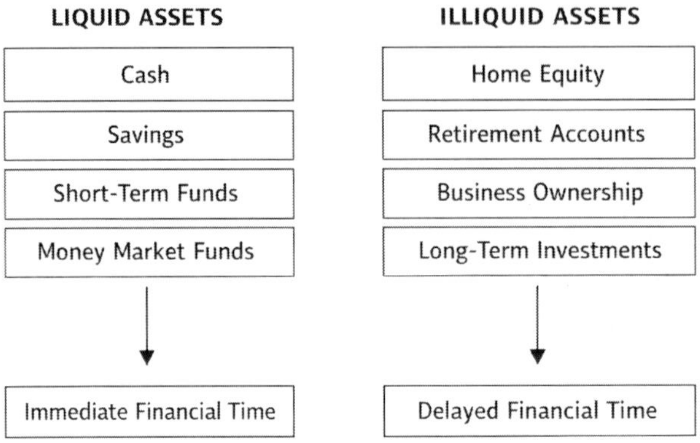

[Diagram 5 — Liquid Assets vs Illiquid Assets]

Financial assets vary widely in how quickly they can be converted into usable funds.

Some assets exist in forms that provide immediate liquidity. Cash balances and accessible savings accounts can be used instantly to meet obligations or absorb financial disturbances. Because these resources require no conversion process, they directly create financial time within the household financial system.

Other assets contain financial value but are slower to access.

Investments, property ownership, and other forms of accumulated wealth may represent significant financial value, yet converting that value into usable liquidity often requires a sequence of actions. These actions may involve transactions, administrative processes, negotiations, or market participation.

During stable periods, these differences in accessibility may seem unimportant.

When income flows regularly and expenses follow predictable schedules, the household may rarely need to convert assets into liquidity quickly. The financial system functions normally because day-to-day obligations are supported by routine cash flow.

However, when disturbances occur, the speed at which assets can produce liquidity becomes critical.

Unexpected expenses, income interruptions, or other financial shocks require immediate resources in order to maintain operational continuity. Assets that cannot quickly provide liquidity may offer little immediate assistance during these periods.

This distinction highlights the difference between financial value and financial time.

Value reflects the total resources contained within the financial system. Liquidity determines how quickly those resources can be used to sustain operations.

A household with substantial value but limited liquidity may appear strong while operating with a narrow stability margin.

The financial system may contain assets capable of supporting long-term financial goals, yet lack the accessible resources required to absorb short-term disturbances.

This condition creates the structural vulnerability known as a liquidity trap.

Liquidity traps often arise when financial value accumulates in assets that are difficult to convert into usable funds within a short period of time.

Many households gradually concentrate wealth in long-term assets. These assets may appreciate over time and contribute significantly to net worth, yet they often provide limited immediate liquidity.

One of the most common examples is home equity.

Residential property frequently represents the largest asset on a household balance sheet. As mortgage balances decline and property values increase, homeowners accumulate equity that appears to strengthen their financial position.

However, accessing that equity usually requires refinancing, borrowing against the property, or selling the home entirely. Each of these processes requires time and may depend on external financial conditions.

As a result, home equity often contains substantial financial value while providing little immediate financial time.

Retirement accounts present another common liquidity trap.

These accounts are designed primarily for long-term financial accumulation. Tax advantages and regulatory structures encourage households to preserve these assets until retirement. Although retirement accounts may contain large balances, accessing them often involves penalties, administrative restrictions, or complex withdrawal procedures.

Concentrated investment positions can produce similar dynamics.

A household may hold significant value in a particular investment or asset class. While the value of the asset may be substantial, converting that position into liquidity may require selling under unfavorable conditions or accepting market prices that fluctuate significantly.

In such cases, the household may hesitate to access the asset even when liquidity is needed.

Business ownership stakes can also function as liquidity traps.

Ownership in a private business may represent a large portion of household wealth. However, converting that ownership into cash may require complex negotiations, external buyers, or structural changes within the business itself.

The process may take months or years rather than days.

In each of these situations, the household appears financially secure when evaluated through total asset value. Yet the financial system may lack the accessible liquidity required to respond quickly to disturbances.

The assets contain value, but they cannot immediately generate financial time.

When households encounter financial disturbances while operating within a liquidity trap, the absence of accessible liquidity can quickly alter the decision environment.

Even when total wealth appears substantial, the household may lack the financial time required to respond gradually to disruption. Obligations continue to arrive according to fixed schedules, yet the resources capable of meeting those obligations may not be readily accessible.

This mismatch creates the conditions that lead to decision compression.

Without sufficient liquidity reserves, households must resolve financial pressure quickly. Assets that contain value may require time to convert into usable funds, but the financial system may not possess that time.

As a result, households may be forced to take rapid actions in order to generate liquidity.

Borrowing becomes a common response.

When assets cannot be converted quickly enough, households may seek external financing to bridge the gap between available liquidity and immediate obligations. Borrowing provides immediate financial resources but introduces new commitments that must be sustained in the future.

In other cases, households may attempt to restructure or liquidate assets quickly.

Rapid asset sales often occur under unfavorable conditions because the household lacks the time required to wait for better opportunities. Financial value may be sacrificed in exchange for immediate liquidity.

These responses reflect the structural constraints created by liquidity traps.

The household possesses financial value, but that value cannot be mobilized quickly enough to support deliberate decision-making. As financial pressure increases, decisions must be made rapidly in order to maintain operational continuity.

The presence of substantial wealth does not eliminate this pressure.

Without accessible liquidity, the system behaves as though those assets were temporarily unavailable. The household must operate within the limits imposed by its liquidity structure rather than by its total financial value.

Liquidity traps therefore illustrate how financial systems can experience instability despite appearing financially strong.

The absence of financial time forces decisions to occur under urgency even when the household's long-term wealth remains substantial.

Stable household financial systems recognize the difference between asset growth and liquidity accessibility.

Assets that accumulate value over time play an important role in long-term financial development. Property ownership, investment portfolios, retirement accounts, and business assets all contribute to the overall financial value of the household.

However, these assets often serve long-duration purposes.

They increase wealth across time but may not provide the immediate liquidity required to sustain operations during financial disturbances. For this reason, stable financial systems typically maintain a balance between long-term assets and accessible liquidity.

This balance ensures that the household possesses resources capable of producing financial time when uncertainty appears.

A dedicated liquidity layer allows the system to absorb disturbances without immediately restructuring long-term assets. Unexpected expenses can be absorbed without selling investments prematurely. Income interruptions can be managed without introducing new financial obligations under pressure.

By preserving accessible liquidity, the household protects its ability to make financial decisions deliberately.

Avoiding liquidity traps therefore requires awareness of how financial value is distributed across different asset categories.

If too much value becomes concentrated in assets that cannot be converted quickly into usable funds, the household may appear wealthy while lacking operational resilience.

Maintaining accessible liquidity ensures that financial value can support the system not only in the long term but also during periods of uncertainty.

Liquidity provides the financial time required to navigate disturbances without destabilizing the household's financial structure.

In this way, liquidity structure becomes a central component of financial stability.

The presence of valuable assets alone does not guarantee resilience. Stability emerges when the financial system contains both long-term value and accessible resources capable of sustaining operations when conditions change.

Liquidity traps therefore reveal an important structural lesson about household financial systems. Accumulating financial value is not sufficient to maintain stability if that value cannot be converted into financial time when uncertainty appears.

Rebuilding Runway

Household financial systems do not remain static. Over time, financial runway may expand or contract as income changes, expenses evolve, and liquidity reserves fluctuate. Disturbances such as income interruptions or expense shocks can reduce financial time rapidly, while gradual changes—such as rising burn rates or liquidity traps—can erode runway quietly.

When runway declines, the stability margin narrows.

At this stage, the household financial system becomes more sensitive to uncertainty. Disturbances that would previously have been absorbed comfortably may begin to produce financial pressure. Rebuilding runway becomes essential for restoring operational stability.

Rebuilding runway means restoring financial time.

The process requires rebalancing the relationship between liquidity and burn rate. Financial time expands when liquidity grows faster than the burn rate.

Two structural adjustments drive this recovery.

First, burn rate must stabilize so that existing liquidity stops eroding rapidly. Second, liquidity reserves must gradually increase so that the system regains operational distance from instability.

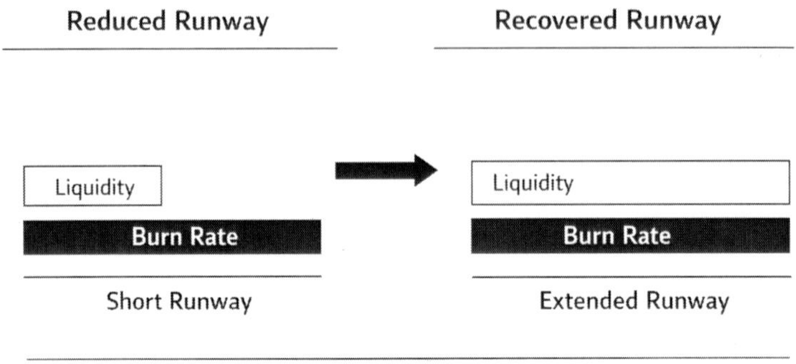

Runway expands when liquidity grows faster than expenses.

[Diagram 6 — Runway Recovery: Burn Rate vs Liquidity]

Together, these adjustments rebuild the stability margin and allow the household financial system to regain its capacity to absorb uncertainty.

The process of rebuilding runway usually begins with recognition.

Because financial stability often erodes gradually, households may not immediately notice that their stability margin has narrowed. Liquidity may still exist within the system, obligations may continue to be met, and the financial structure may appear stable in the present moment.

Yet beneath the surface, financial time may be declining.

Expense shocks are one of the most visible causes. Unexpected costs such as repairs or medical obligations consume liquidity immediately. When these disturbances occur, the household's financial reserves decline and the financial runway shortens.

Income interruptions create similar effects.

When income stops temporarily, liquidity reserves begin to sustain the system's expenses. As those reserves are consumed, financial runway declines.

Lifestyle expansion can produce a more gradual form of runway loss.

As recurring expenses increase over time, the burn rate of the financial system rises. Even if liquidity remains unchanged, higher expenses shorten the amount of time those reserves can sustain the system during uncertainty.

Liquidity traps represent another source of erosion.

When wealth accumulates in assets that cannot easily be converted into usable liquidity, the household may possess financial value but lack accessible resources capable of producing financial time. During disturbances, the absence of liquidity becomes visible as the system struggles to sustain operations.

Each of these mechanisms reduces the stability margin.

Because the erosion may occur slowly or invisibly, recognizing the loss of financial time becomes the first step in restoring stability.

Runway provides a useful lens for observing this change.

By measuring how long the household can sustain operations under uncertainty, runway shows whether the stability margin is expanding or contracting. A declining runway indicates that the financial system has moved closer to the threshold of instability.

Recognition of this shift allows the household to begin rebuilding financial time before disturbances escalate further.

Once runway loss has been recognized, the first structural adjustment often involves stabilizing the household's burn rate.

Burn rate determines how quickly liquidity is consumed when income becomes uncertain. Because it defines the speed of the financial system, changes in burn rate have a direct effect on the amount of financial time available within the system.

When burn rate rises, financial runway shortens.

Rebuilding runway therefore frequently begins with preventing further expansion of expenses.

This does not necessarily require eliminating all discretionary spending or making abrupt lifestyle changes. Instead, the focus lies on understanding which expenses represent structural commitments within the financial system.

Structural expenses include obligations that must be sustained regardless of short-term financial conditions.

Housing commitments, long-term service contracts, insurance obligations, and recurring financial arrangements often define the baseline burn rate of the household system. These expenses determine how much liquidity is required to sustain operations during uncertainty.

When burn rate grows faster than liquidity reserves, financial runway erodes.

Stabilizing burn rate therefore slows the consumption of liquidity and preserves the financial time that remains within the system.

Even modest adjustments can extend runway meaningfully.

Consider a household with $12,000 in liquidity and a monthly burn rate of $4,000.

Runway = 3 months.

If structural expenses are adjusted so that the burn rate declines to $3,500 per month, the same liquidity now produces a longer operational horizon.

$12,000 liquidity

÷ $3,500 burn rate

Runway ≈ 3.4 months

Although the adjustment appears small, the system gains additional financial time without increasing liquidity reserves.

Stabilizing burn rate therefore increases the efficiency with which liquidity produces financial time.

This adjustment represents one half of the runway recovery process.

By slowing the pace at which liquidity is consumed, the household preserves the remaining stability margin while rebuilding reserves.

Stabilizing burn rate slows the erosion of financial time, but restoring a wider stability margin also requires rebuilding liquidity reserves.

Liquidity reserves represent the accessible resources that sustain the household financial system during periods of uncertainty. When disturbances consume these reserves, the system loses operational time.

Rebuilding liquidity gradually restores that time.

This process typically occurs through several channels.

Income recovery is often the first contributor. When income resumes after an interruption, the household financial system begins to generate resources that can replenish depleted liquidity.

Savings accumulation can also contribute to reserve rebuilding.

When income exceeds expenses, the difference gradually increases liquidity reserves. Over time, this accumulation expands the financial runway.

Other financial adjustments may also support the rebuilding process.

Asset restructuring, improved income stability, or disciplined reserve rebuilding strategies may all contribute to the restoration of liquidity reserves.

The critical factor is the relationship between liquidity growth and the burn rate.

Runway expands when liquidity increases faster than expenses.

Consider a household with $9,000 in liquidity and a burn rate of $3,000 per month.

Runway equals three months.

If liquidity reserves gradually increase to $12,000 while burn rate remains unchanged, the household's financial runway expands.

$12,000 liquidity

÷ $3,000 burn rate

Runway = 4 months

The stability margin has widened.

This gradual expansion restores the system's capacity to absorb future disturbances without destabilizing.

The process often occurs incrementally as the household restores balance within its financial structure. Over time, steady increases in reserves rebuild the financial time that protects the system from uncertainty.

The goal is not immediate recovery but sustained expansion of liquidity relative to burn rate.

Rebuilding runway restores financial time, but maintaining stability requires ongoing attention to the relationship between liquidity and burn rate.

This ongoing oversight can be described as liquidity governance.

Liquidity governance involves monitoring the structure of the household financial system and ensuring that liquidity reserves remain aligned with the system's burn rate. By observing this relationship, households can detect gradual erosion of financial time before it becomes destabilizing.

Without this awareness, runway can quietly decline.

Lifestyle expansion may increase expenses, financial commitments may accumulate, and liquidity reserves may fail to grow at the same pace. Over time, the stability margin may narrow without producing immediate financial pressure.

When disturbances eventually occur, the household may discover that its operational horizon has diminished.

Liquidity governance helps prevent this outcome by maintaining visibility into the financial system's stability margin.

Households that monitor runway periodically can observe whether financial time is expanding or contracting. Adjustments to expenses or liquidity reserves can then be made before the system approaches instability.

This perspective reframes financial management.

Instead of focusing solely on income or savings balances, households observe how structural expenses interact with liquidity reserves to produce financial time.

Runway becomes a structural metric within the financial system.

Rebuilding runway therefore represents more than a recovery from disruption.

It represents the restoration of a stable relationship between burn rate and liquidity—a relationship that produces sufficient financial time to absorb uncertainty.

Maintaining this relationship ensures that the stability margin remains wide enough to protect the household financial system from future disturbances.

Rebuilding runway therefore restores the operational stability of the household financial system. Liquidity reserves expand, burn rate stabilizes, and the system regains the financial time required to absorb uncertainty. However, stability created through recovery must be preserved through ongoing management.

Managing Liquidity as a System

Rebuilding financial runway restores stability to a household financial system. When liquidity reserves expand and burn rate stabilizes, the system regains financial time and the stability margin widens. Disturbances can once again be absorbed without immediately threatening the household's ability to sustain its obligations.

However, recovered financial runway does not guarantee permanent stability.

Household financial systems continue to evolve. Income levels change, expenses adjust, and assets accumulate in different forms. Without ongoing attention to these dynamics, the financial time that was once rebuilt can gradually erode again.

Maintaining stability therefore requires the deliberate management of liquidity.

Liquidity governance refers to the ongoing process through which households monitor the relationship between liquidity reserves, burn rate, and financial runway. Rather than allowing liquidity to fluctuate passively, stable financial systems treat liquidity as a structural resource that must be preserved.

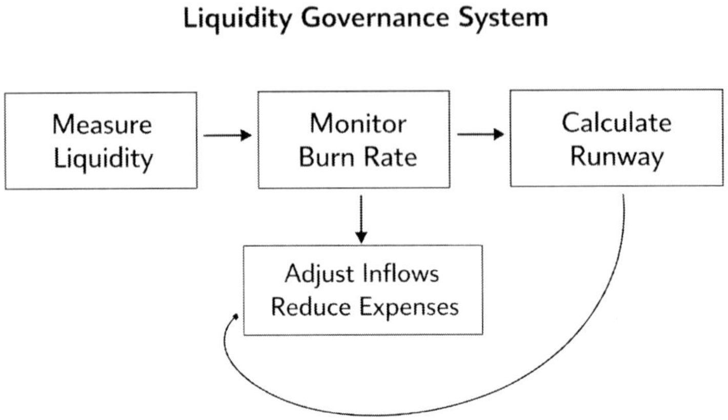

Stability is maintained through continuous adjustment.

[Diagram 7 — Liquidity Governance Cycle]

Through liquidity governance, households maintain awareness of the stability margin within their financial systems, ensuring that financial time remains available when uncertainty appears.

In many household financial systems, liquidity emerges as an incidental by-product of income and spending patterns.

Funds accumulate when income exceeds expenses and decline when expenses increase or disturbances occur. Liquidity balances fluctuate as financial activity unfolds. Because these changes often occur gradually, households may treat liquidity as a passive outcome of financial life rather than as a resource requiring deliberate management.

However, liquidity performs a structural role within the financial system.

It allows the household to sustain operations during uncertainty and provides the space required for deliberate financial decision-making. Without sufficient liquidity, the system loses operational flexibility and becomes vulnerable to disturbances.

For this reason, stable financial systems treat liquidity as a managed resource rather than as an accidental balance.

Managing liquidity involves recognizing that the availability of financial time depends on how liquidity interacts with the household's burn rate. When expenses increase or when liquidity becomes concentrated in illiquid assets, the amount of financial time available within the system declines.

These changes may occur even when the household appears financially strong.

Income may grow and assets may accumulate, yet the financial system may gradually lose liquidity if resources are directed primarily toward long-term investments or lifestyle expansion. Over time, the system may possess substantial wealth while simultaneously holding limited accessible liquidity.

Liquidity governance addresses this structural risk.

By treating liquidity as an essential component of the financial system, households ensure that financial time remains available. Liquidity reserves are maintained deliberately rather than allowed to fluctuate unpredictably.

This perspective reframes liquidity.

Instead of viewing liquid reserves as idle capital that could be deployed elsewhere, liquidity is recognized as a structural element that supports the stability of the financial system. It provides the financial time required to navigate uncertainty.

When liquidity is managed intentionally, the household preserves the financial time necessary to maintain control over its financial decisions.

Liquidity governance requires ongoing awareness of the stability margin within the household financial system.

The stability margin reflects the distance between the present financial structure and the point where obligations can no longer be sustained. This margin is determined by the interaction of three elements: burn rate, liquidity reserves, and financial runway.

Monitoring this relationship allows households to observe how the stability margin evolves over time.

Burn rate defines the speed at which liquidity is consumed during periods of uncertainty. Liquidity reserves represent the resources that sustain operations when income becomes uncertain. Together, these elements determine the length of financial runway.

When burn rate rises while liquidity remains unchanged, financial runway shortens and the stability margin narrows.

When liquidity increases faster than expenses, runway expands and the stability margin widens.

Liquidity governance involves periodic observation of these relationships.

Households assess whether changes in expenses, income, or asset allocation have altered the balance between burn rate and liquidity reserves. Even modest shifts in these variables can influence the operational horizon of the financial system.

For example, a household may experience gradual increases in recurring expenses as lifestyle patterns evolve. Housing costs, service commitments, and other obligations may accumulate over time. Each increase in burn rate reduces the amount of financial time produced by existing liquidity reserves.

If liquidity governance is absent, this erosion may go unnoticed.

The household continues meeting its obligations, and the financial system appears stable in the present moment. However, the stability margin may be narrowing quietly.

By monitoring the relationship between burn rate and liquidity reserves, households can recognize this shift before financial pressure appears.

Early recognition allows adjustments to occur gradually. Expenses can be stabilized, liquidity reserves can be strengthened, and the stability margin can be restored before disturbances escalate.

Liquidity governance functions as an early warning system within the household financial structure.

It ensures that the stability margin remains visible rather than allowing financial time to erode unnoticed.

The central purpose of liquidity governance is the preservation of financial time.

Financial time allows households to respond to uncertainty deliberately rather than reactively. When liquidity reserves are sufficient, disturbances such as income interruptions or expense shocks can be absorbed without immediately threatening the household's operational stability.

This preservation of financial time protects decision quality.

When the stability margin is wide, households have the ability to evaluate financial situations carefully before responding. Decisions can be made with consideration of long-term consequences rather than under immediate pressure.

In contrast, when financial time disappears, the household enters an environment where decisions must be made quickly.

Urgent obligations compress the decision horizon, forcing households to prioritize immediate survival over long-term stability. Financial choices made in these conditions often introduce new constraints that affect the system later.

Liquidity governance helps prevent this transition.

By maintaining liquidity reserves and monitoring the relationship between expenses and reserves, households ensure that financial time remains available within the system. Disturbances can occur without immediately pushing the household toward decision compression.

Operationally, the household retains the ability to sustain its obligations during uncertainty. Behaviorally, it retains the cognitive space required to evaluate financial decisions carefully.

These two forms of stability reinforce one another.

When financial time exists, households can respond to disturbances in ways that preserve the long-term structure of the financial system. When financial time disappears, the urgency of the moment often drives decisions that weaken the system further.

Financial stability is not a fixed state achieved once and then permanently secured. Household financial systems evolve continuously as income changes, assets accumulate, and lifestyles adjust.

Because of this constant evolution, maintaining stability requires ongoing governance.

Liquidity governance provides the framework through which households maintain alignment between liquidity reserves and the structural expenses that define burn rate. As the financial system grows or changes, this relationship must be observed and managed deliberately.

Without such governance, financial time can erode gradually.

Lifestyle expansion may increase expenses faster than liquidity grows. Investments may concentrate wealth in illiquid assets that cannot easily produce financial time. Over extended periods, the stability margin may narrow even as the household's total financial value increases.

This erosion can occur quietly.

The household may appear financially successful in terms of income, assets, or net worth, yet possess limited operational resilience when disturbances occur. Financial time may have diminished even while financial value has grown.

Liquidity governance addresses this risk by maintaining a structural focus on financial time.

By periodically observing burn rate, liquidity reserves, and runway, households maintain visibility into the stability margin of their financial systems. Adjustments can be made before financial pressure emerges.

This practice transforms liquidity management from a reactive process into a proactive one.

Rather than rebuilding runway only after disturbances occur, households maintain the conditions that preserve financial time continuously.

In this way, liquidity governance supports long-term stability.

It ensures that the household financial system retains the operational flexibility required to navigate uncertainty without destabilizing the structure that supports long-term financial development.

Liquidity governance preserves the financial time required for stability, but overall resilience ultimately depends on how the entire structure supports that time.

Stability Under Stress

Economic conditions do not remain stable. Periods of expansion are regularly followed by periods of contraction, and changes in employment conditions, income stability, and asset values ripple through household financial systems. These cycles introduce stress that tests the resilience of the structures households have built to sustain their financial lives.

External disruptions during these periods can take many forms. Employment opportunities may decline, income streams may become uncertain, and asset values may fluctuate. Financial commitments that once appeared manageable may become more difficult to sustain as economic conditions shift.

These conditions do not affect all households in the same way.

The degree to which a household experiences financial instability during economic stress depends largely on the strength of its stability margin. Households with sufficient financial runway possess the financial time necessary to adapt to changing conditions. Households operating with narrow margins may experience immediate financial pressure as external disruptions appear.

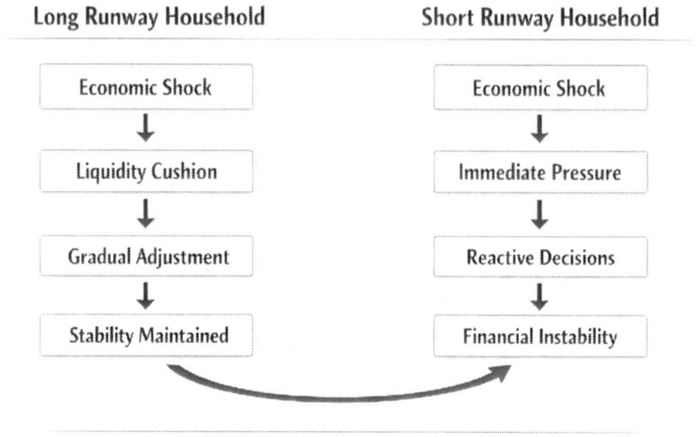

Runway determines how households experience economic stress.

[Diagram 8 — Economic Stress and Financial Runway]

Economic stress therefore acts as a test of the household financial system. The strength of liquidity reserves and the length of financial runway determine whether the system absorbs these disturbances gradually or encounters rapid destabilization.

Household financial systems exist within broader economic environments. When those environments change, households experience the effects through disruptions to income, employment stability, and asset values.

Economic downturns frequently increase the volatility of income.

Employment opportunities may become less predictable as businesses adjust to declining demand. Organizations may reduce staffing levels, working hours, or compensation structures in response to changing conditions. Even households with historically stable income streams may encounter unexpected interruptions.

Contract-based and variable income arrangements can become particularly sensitive to economic shifts.

Periods between projects may lengthen, new work opportunities may become more difficult to secure, and income variability may increase. Households that rely on these forms of income may experience sudden fluctuations in financial inflows.

Asset values can also change during periods of economic stress.

Financial markets may decline, property values may stagnate or fall, and business revenues may fluctuate. While these changes primarily affect long-term financial value, they can influence household behavior if assets must be accessed to support operations.

In combination, these factors introduce disturbances into household financial systems.

Income becomes less predictable, financial opportunities may narrow, and uncertainty increases. The system must continue meeting its obligations while adapting to these changes.

During these periods, liquidity reserves become the primary mechanism through which households maintain operational continuity.

The ability to sustain expenses while income adjusts or recovers depends largely on the availability of accessible financial resources. Liquidity allows the household to continue operating even as external conditions fluctuate.

Without sufficient liquidity, economic stress can quickly propagate through the household financial system.

Obligations remain constant while income becomes uncertain, creating immediate pressure on the financial structure. Households may be forced to respond rapidly to maintain operational continuity.

The difference between these outcomes often depends on the stability margin available within the system.

Economic stress does not create instability on its own. Rather, it reveals how resilient the household financial structure is when external conditions become uncertain.

During periods of economic stress, liquidity buffers function as the primary shock absorbers within the household financial system.

When income becomes uncertain or employment conditions change, the household must rely on existing resources to sustain its financial obligations. Liquidity reserves provide the resources that allow the system to continue operating as these disruptions unfold.

The role of liquidity becomes particularly visible during economic downturns.

As employment instability increases or income flows fluctuate, households must maintain their essential expenses even when financial inflows become irregular. Liquidity allows the system to absorb this temporary imbalance between income and expenses.

This absorption process slows the propagation of financial shocks.

Without liquidity buffers, disturbances move quickly through the financial structure. Income interruptions immediately threaten the ability to meet obligations, and financial pressure increases rapidly as expenses continue to arrive.

With liquidity buffers, the household possesses a layer of protection.

Accessible reserves allow expenses to be sustained while the system adjusts to new conditions. The household can maintain operational continuity while exploring alternative income opportunities or adapting to changes in the economic environment.

This shock absorption function is particularly important during periods of widespread economic stress.

When many households experience similar disruptions simultaneously, employment markets may become more competitive and recovery periods may lengthen. Liquidity reserves provide the time necessary to navigate these conditions without immediate destabilization.

Liquidity therefore determines how economic stress is experienced within the household system.

Households with strong liquidity buffers can absorb disturbances gradually. The financial system remains operational while adjustments occur over time.

Households with limited liquidity may experience the same disturbances as immediate crises. Without accessible reserves, the system lacks the resources required to maintain stability during the adjustment period.

Liquidity does not eliminate economic stress, but it changes how the system responds to it.

By absorbing shocks at the moment they occur, liquidity preserves the operational continuity of the household financial structure.

Financial runway determines how gradually households can adapt to changing economic conditions.

When economic stress disrupts income or employment, the household must respond to the new environment. Adaptation may involve searching for new employment, restructuring income arrangements, adjusting expenses, or renegotiating financial commitments.

These adjustments require time.

Financial runway provides this time.

Households with longer runway possess a larger financial horizon between the present moment and the point where obligations can no longer be sustained. This horizon allows them to respond to economic disruptions deliberately rather than urgently.

For example, when employment is interrupted, households with substantial runway can conduct a careful search for new opportunities. They can evaluate potential positions based on long-term suitability rather than accepting the first available option.

Similarly, households may reorganize expenses gradually as they observe how economic conditions evolve.

Longer runway also allows households to restructure commitments when necessary. Obligations may be renegotiated, expenses adjusted, or financial arrangements reorganized in ways that preserve the long-term stability of the system.

In contrast, households with limited runway face a compressed adaptation process.

Because financial time is scarce, adjustments must occur quickly. Employment decisions may be made under pressure, expenses may be reduced abruptly, and financial commitments may be altered rapidly in order to sustain operations.

These rapid adjustments often occur without the benefit of full information.

Economic conditions may still be evolving, yet the household must act immediately because the financial system lacks the time required for careful evaluation.

Runway therefore determines the pace at which households adapt to economic change.

Longer runway allows adaptation to occur gradually and deliberately. Short runway forces rapid adjustments that may introduce additional instability into the financial system.

The presence of financial time transforms economic stress from an immediate threat into a condition that can be navigated.

During periods of economic stress, the stability margin of the household financial system becomes especially important.

The stability margin represents the operational distance between the present financial structure and the point where obligations can no longer be sustained. This distance determines how resilient the system remains when external conditions become uncertain.

Households with wider stability margins possess greater resilience.

Because financial runway is longer, disturbances must accumulate over a longer period before the system approaches instability. The household can continue meeting its obligations while adapting to the changing economic environment.

This resilience allows the financial structure to remain intact.

Long-term assets do not need to be liquidated prematurely, and financial commitments do not require immediate restructuring. The household can maintain its broader financial strategy while navigating temporary economic disruptions.

In contrast, households with narrow stability margins operate close to the threshold of instability.

When economic stress appears, the system may approach this threshold quickly. Even modest income interruptions or financial disturbances can reduce the remaining runway to a point where obligations become difficult to sustain.

This proximity to instability increases the likelihood of rapid financial adjustments.

Assets may need to be converted into liquidity quickly, borrowing may become necessary, and financial commitments may require abrupt restructuring. Each of these responses attempts to preserve operational continuity but may introduce new constraints into the financial system.

The stability margin therefore determines how households experience economic uncertainty.

When the margin is wide, disturbances remain manageable. When the margin is narrow, the same disturbances may produce immediate financial pressure.

Financial runway is the mechanism that creates this margin.

By providing financial time, liquidity reserves allow the household to absorb uncertainty without destabilizing its long-term financial structure.

During economic stress, this financial time becomes one of the most important resources within the system.

When financial time is preserved, households retain the ability to navigate uncertainty without destabilizing their long-term financial structure. This insight leads to the central idea that underlies the entire framework presented in this book.

Financial Time and Decision Freedom

Throughout this book, liquidity has been examined primarily as a structural component of household financial systems. Liquidity sustains operations during uncertainty, absorbs disturbances, and preserves the stability margin that separates the present financial structure from instability.

Yet the ultimate benefit of liquidity extends beyond financial survival.

Liquidity creates financial time. This time allows households to evaluate choices rather than responding immediately to financial pressure. Instead of making decisions under urgency, households with sufficient financial time can observe changing conditions, compare alternatives, and respond deliberately.

Financial stability therefore produces something more valuable than simply meeting obligations.

It produces decision freedom.

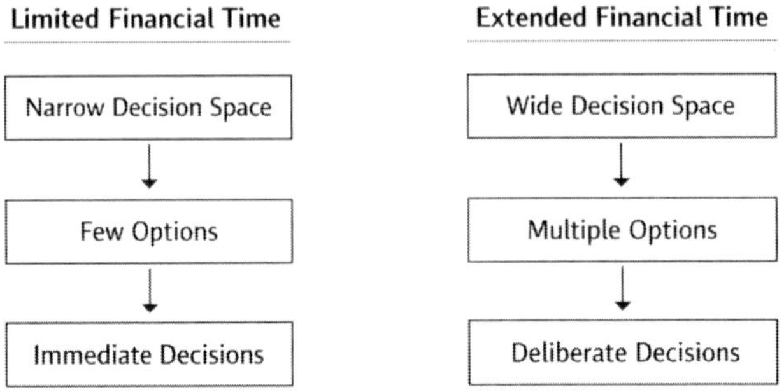

Financial time expands optionality.

[Diagram 9 — Financial Time and Decision Space]

Most discussions of personal finance focus on quantities of money.

Income levels, account balances, asset values, and net worth are commonly used to evaluate financial strength. These measurements describe the resources contained within a household financial system and often serve as indicators of financial progress.

However, these measurements alone do not explain how a financial system behaves during uncertainty.

Two households with identical income and similar asset values may experience very different outcomes when financial disturbances occur. One household may absorb disruption gradually, while the other may encounter immediate pressure that forces rapid financial adjustments.

The difference lies not in the amount of money available but in the amount of time that money can produce.

Financial time represents a hidden dimension of financial stability.

Financial disturbances unfold across time. Income interruptions may last weeks or months before employment is restored. Unexpected expenses may require immediate payment while financial adjustments take longer to implement. Economic downturns may alter financial conditions gradually before recovery occurs.

During these periods, the household financial system must continue operating.

Liquidity converts financial resources into the time required to sustain this process. Accessible liquidity allows the household to meet obligations while evaluating how to respond to changing circumstances.

Without this liquidity, the system loses financial time.

Obligations continue to arrive on schedule, but the household lacks the resources required to sustain operations while solutions are developed. Financial decisions must occur immediately because the system cannot continue operating without rapid adjustment.

Understanding finance through the lens of time reveals a different perspective on stability.

Financial strength is not determined solely by the quantity of resources within the system. It is determined by how much time those resources create when uncertainty appears.

Liquidity therefore acts as the mechanism that transforms financial value into time.

This time determines how the household navigates uncertainty.

When financial time disappears, the decision environment of the household changes dramatically.

Without sufficient liquidity, the household's ability to sustain its obligations becomes dependent on immediate financial adjustments. Income interruptions, expense shocks, or economic disruptions quickly place pressure on the financial structure because the system lacks the resources required to absorb those disturbances gradually.

This environment produces decision compression.

Decision compression occurs when the available time for evaluating financial choices disappears. Instead of comparing alternatives carefully, households must resolve financial pressure quickly in order to maintain operational continuity.

Under these conditions, the decision horizon narrows.

Financial choices become constrained by urgency. The household must prioritize immediate survival rather than long-term stability because obligations must be met within a limited timeframe.

The range of viable alternatives becomes smaller.

Options that require time to develop may no longer be available because the financial system cannot sustain the delay required to pursue them. Employment opportunities must be accepted quickly, financial commitments may need to be renegotiated rapidly, and assets may need to be converted into liquidity under unfavorable conditions.

These decisions are not necessarily irrational.

They represent the structural consequences of operating within a system that lacks financial time.

When liquidity disappears, the household must respond immediately to financial pressure. Decisions that would normally be evaluated carefully must instead be made quickly because the system cannot sustain operations long enough for deliberate evaluation.

Decision compression constrains the household's ability to choose among alternatives.

The absence of financial time reduces optionality.

Instead of selecting the most advantageous option, the household may be forced to select whichever option resolves the immediate problem. The financial system becomes reactive rather than deliberate.

This constraint illustrates why liquidity plays such an important role in financial stability.

Liquidity preserves financial time, and financial time protects the decision environment in which financial choices occur.

Financial runway expands the range of options available within the household financial system.

When runway is long, the household possesses an extended operational horizon between the present moment and the point where obligations can no longer be sustained. This horizon allows the household to evaluate multiple responses to changing conditions.

Runway increases decision optionality.

Optionality refers to the ability to choose among several possible courses of action rather than being forced into a single response by immediate constraints.

Households with longer runway can explore alternatives before committing to decisions.

When employment disruptions occur, these households can search for opportunities that align with their long-term goals rather than accepting the first available option. They can evaluate the stability of potential income sources and consider how each choice affects their broader financial structure.

Similarly, financial restructuring can occur gradually.

Expenses may be adjusted in stages rather than through abrupt changes. Financial commitments can be renegotiated thoughtfully rather than under immediate pressure.

Runway also allows households to respond to economic change with patience.

When external conditions shift, households with sufficient financial time can observe how those conditions evolve before making significant adjustments. This observational period allows them to respond with greater clarity.

In contrast, households with limited runway possess fewer options.

Because the operational horizon of the financial system is short, decisions must be made quickly. The household may not have the time required to explore multiple alternatives or wait for favorable opportunities.

Optionality disappears as the stability margin narrows.

The financial system becomes constrained by time pressure, and the range of possible responses shrinks accordingly.

Runway therefore acts as a structural source of flexibility within the household financial system.

The more financial time the system contains, the greater the number of viable choices available to the household.

The ultimate purpose of liquidity and runway is not simply the preservation of financial obligations.

Their deeper function is the preservation of decision freedom.

Financial systems exist within environments of uncertainty. Income flows fluctuate, expenses occasionally increase unexpectedly, and economic conditions change over time. The household must continuously adapt to these conditions while maintaining the structure that supports its financial life.

Liquidity provides the time required to navigate this uncertainty.

When financial time exists within the system, households retain the ability to evaluate alternatives and choose responses deliberately. Decisions can be made with awareness of long-term consequences rather than solely in response to immediate financial pressure.

This freedom shapes the trajectory of the financial system.

Households with sufficient runway can pursue opportunities aligned with their goals, adjust their financial structures gradually, and respond to disturbances without destabilizing the system that supports their long-term plans.

In contrast, households operating without financial time experience constrained decision environments.

Financial pressure forces rapid responses, reducing the range of available alternatives. Decisions may resolve immediate problems but introduce new constraints that shape the financial system in unintended ways.

Over time, the difference between these environments becomes significant.

One system operates with deliberation and flexibility. The other operates under urgency and constraint.

Liquidity determines which decision environment prevails.

By converting financial resources into operational time, liquidity preserves the ability of households to navigate uncertainty without sacrificing long-term stability.

Financial time therefore becomes the foundation of sustainable financial systems.

It allows households not only to survive disturbances but also to maintain control over the choices that shape their financial future.

Understanding this relationship between liquidity, time, and decision freedom reveals the central insight of the framework presented throughout this book.

The Quiet Power of Financial Time

Financial stability is often associated with the accumulation of wealth. Discussions of financial strength frequently focus on income levels, investment performance, and the size of a household's assets. These measures appear to capture the household's financial position at a particular moment.

Yet the deeper source of financial stability is not simply the amount of wealth a household possesses.

Stability depends on the amount of financial time the household has to respond when uncertainty appears.

Income may fluctuate. Expenses may arise unexpectedly. Economic conditions may shift. These disturbances are a normal feature of financial life. What determines whether they remain manageable or become destabilizing is the amount of time available to adapt.

Liquidity creates that time.

By converting financial resources into operational duration, liquidity allows the household financial system to continue functioning while uncertainty unfolds. In this way, the quiet foundation of stability is not simply wealth itself, but the financial time that wealth can produce.

Households often evaluate their financial position by examining income and assets. These measurements provide visible indicators of financial progress. Higher income suggests greater financial capacity, and larger asset balances appear to indicate increasing security.

However, these measurements do not fully explain financial stability. The defining feature of stability is the ability of the household financial system to continue operating while conditions change. When disturbances appear, the system must sustain its obligations while adapting to new circumstances.

This adaptation requires time.

Income interruptions may require weeks or months before employment stabilizes. Unexpected expenses may temporarily alter the financial structure while solutions are developed. Economic conditions may evolve gradually before returning to equilibrium.

During these periods, the household must continue meeting its obligations. Financial time allows this process to unfold.

When sufficient liquidity exists, the household can sustain operations while responding to change. Obligations continue to be met while the household evaluates how to adapt its financial structure.

Without financial time, the system becomes structurally fragile.

Even small disturbances can threaten the household's ability to maintain its obligations because the system lacks the financial time required to adjust.

Liquidity therefore performs a fundamental role within the financial system.

It converts financial resources into the financial time necessary for adaptation.

Financial stability begins with this capacity to sustain operations while uncertainty unfolds.

Financial runway measures the amount of financial time available within the household system.

This time expands the space in which decisions can occur.

When runway is long, households possess the operational distance required to observe conditions before responding. Financial choices can be evaluated with consideration of long-term consequences rather than made under immediate pressure.

The presence of runway therefore preserves decision freedom.

Households with sufficient financial time can compare alternatives and choose responses that align with their broader financial goals. Employment decisions, financial restructuring, and lifestyle adjustments can occur gradually rather than abruptly.

This deliberate pace protects the system's stability margin.

When disturbances occur, the household remains far from the point where obligations can no longer be sustained. The system absorbs shocks without immediately forcing disruptive changes.

Without financial runway, the decision environment changes.

As liquidity declines and financial time disappears, the household must respond quickly to maintain operational continuity. Decisions become compressed, and the range of viable alternatives narrows.

The objective shifts from choosing the most advantageous option to resolving immediate financial pressure.

Runway therefore protects the space in which financial decisions occur.

It allows households to respond deliberately rather than reactively.

The influence of financial time is often subtle.

Liquidity rarely draws attention in periods of stability. When income flows regularly and expenses remain predictable, liquidity reserves may remain unused. Because these resources are rarely called upon, their importance can appear secondary to income or asset accumulation.

Yet liquidity quietly supports the resilience of the household financial system.

When disturbances appear, liquidity provides the time necessary for the system to respond. Unexpected expenses can be absorbed without destabilizing the financial structure. Income interruptions can be navigated while new opportunities are pursued. Economic uncertainty can be observed without forcing immediate financial restructuring.

Financial time allows households to adapt.

It preserves the ability to respond thoughtfully to change rather than reacting under pressure. This capacity for deliberate adaptation supports the long-term stability of the financial system.

Over time, the quiet presence of financial time shapes the trajectory of the household financial structure.

Households with sufficient financial time can navigate uncertainty while preserving their broader financial goals. Households without financial time may find themselves responding rapidly to disturbances that gradually reshape their financial systems.

The difference lies not only in wealth, but in financial time.

Financial stability does not begin with the accumulation of assets alone.

It begins with the time required to adapt when uncertainty appears.

Liquidity creates that financial time.

About the Author

Mark Ellison writes about structural durability in systems exposed to volatility.

His work focuses on long-horizon stability across financial architecture, career positioning, cognitive resilience, and physical capacity. Rather than treating these domains as separate disciplines, he approaches them as interdependent systems governed by load, margin, buffer depth, and threshold behavior.

The Stability framework examines how fragility accumulates gradually and how disciplined structural calibration preserves optionality across decades. The objective is not optimization for peak outcomes, but preservation of functional continuity under variance.

Money Stability is part of a broader multi-domain stability ecosystem developed under Perennial Publishing, each domain addressing a distinct vector of long-term durability.

The work is designed for readers who prefer structural clarity over motivational rhetoric and long-horizon coherence over short-term intensity.

The Money Stability Series

Money Stability*: How to Build Financial Control in an Unstable World* (Cornerstone Volume)

Liquidity and Runway: *How to Build Financial Time, Extend Your Runway, and Stay Stable in an Unstable Economy*

Future Titles include:
Income Stability
Expense Stability

Part of a Broader Stability Framework

The Money Stability Series is part of a larger stability ecosystem published by Perennial Publishing.

Related domains include:

Metabolic Stability — biological load, energy, and recovery capacity

Career Stability — income durability, positioning, and transition resilience

Mental Stability — cognitive steadiness under pressure and uncertainty

Emotional Stability — regulatory steadiness in environments that do not slow down

Each domain approaches stability as a structural problem: capacity versus load, buffers versus shocks, and governance versus drift. Together, they form a unified framework for long-horizon durability across the major systems that determine life trajectory.

About Perennial Publishing

Perennial Publishing produces practical systems guides for building stability in an unstable world.

Our books explore the foundations of long-term resilience across health, finance, career, and everyday decision-making. Each title focuses on clear frameworks, durable principles, and practical strategies that help readers build lasting stability rather than short-term fixes.

The Perennial catalog includes series on metabolic health, financial stability, career systems, and personal consistency. While each book stands on its own, they share a common goal: helping individuals create durable systems that support a stable and sustainable life.

For bulk or institutional orders, contact Perennial Publishing.

Made in United States
North Haven, CT
04 November 2026

21768652R00104

Most financial advice focuses on what to do with money once you have it. Very little explains how to stay stable when income is uncertain, expenses are fixed, and time is working against you.

Liquidity and runway are what determine whether pressure becomes a problem—or remains manageable.

This book reframes personal finance as a system of time, access, and control.

Instead of chasing optimization, it focuses on stability:

- How liquidity actually functions under real-world constraints
- Why runway—not income—is the true measure of financial breathing room
- Where most systems break under pressure
- How to build structures that hold when conditions change

No shortcuts. No assumptions of perfect behavior. Just a clear model of how financial stability is built—and how it's lost.

This is not a budgeting guide or an investment playbook. It is a systems-level approach to staying operational in an unstable environment.

For bulk or institutional orders, contact Perennial Publishing.

ISBN 9781971996127
90000
9 781971 996127